(De Santiago Family Publishing)
ISBN-13: 978-0692160381
ISBN-10: 0692160388

For The Queen of Peace

Table of Contents

Chapter 1: JUANITO   4
Chapter 2: THE REQUIEM   15
Chapter 3: THE FAITHFUL DEPARTED   19
Chapter 4: BOBBY   26
Chapter 5: "KNOWLEDGE"   31
Chapter 6: "HEAL MY PEOPLE"   40
Chapter 8: MY GREATEST GIFT   53
Chapter 8: JUANA   69
Chapter 9: CONFIRMATION   77
Chapter 10: SUPERNATURAL EMPATHY   83
Chapter 11: THE SUPERNATURAL   89
Chapter 12: MEDJUGORJE   96
Chapter 13: DARK NIGHT OF THE SOUL   116
Chapter 14: DREAM VISIONS   120
Chapter 15: OUR LADY   128
Chapter 16: PRAYER   136
Chapter 17: THE DARK SIDE   142
Chapter 18: FINAL THOUGHTS   146
ACKNOWLEDGEMENTS   151

Chapter 1: Juanito

Juan Estevan De Santiago was born on October 29, 1965. He was my oldest brother and the oldest sibling of my family of 5 boys and 2 girls.

My brother passed from this world to our Heavenly Father on October 14, 2017. That was the most difficult day in our family's lives.

His life was a complicated and hard one. He made choices that were less than exemplary. Despite all his flaws, my brother had a good heart.

During his viewing, many people came up to the family and told us many accounts of his good will and unselfishness. It was so amazing to see how many lives my brother touched. The outpouring of love for my brother was on full display during those dark days for my family.

These "spiritual gifts" that the Lord has granted me, made the days leading up to his death and after, very hard on me.

I received a vision about a week or so before my brother Juan passed. In the vision, the moving images of seeing my brother in a coffin flashed through my mind. The strange thing though, is that I "saw" my second oldest brother in the coffin and not my brother Juan. I rebuked the vision when it occurred and I prayed as I do when I "receive" things of this sort. I didn't put much thought into it after that because I thought it was perhaps not a true vision since I didn't "feel" death at the time.

I've "received" visions of people I knew in coffins before, and I have usually "felt" death in those situations. It's not always the case but a lot of times it is.

During one of our weekly Charismatic prayers meetings I use to attend with my parents and some of my family, I "received" a strong vision of this sort. The vision was of one of the music leaders. I "saw" him clearly in a coffin. I "received" the typical feeling of death as well. The strong feeling of death approaching was intense. My soul was ripped apart as it was in those days when I "received" an impending death from Above. I "received" the "knowledge" though, that seeing the music leader in the coffin didn't represent his death but a death of someone close to him.

I prayed very fervently that night for his soul and for those close to him. I prayed the Divine Mercy Chaplet, which seemed endlessly for them after that. I continued to pray it with much fervor. I kept praying because the death "feeling" kept lingering the days after the prayer meeting.

The following week at the prayer meeting, the music leader, gave us the news that his mother was gravely ill. We prayed for her that night but I "knew" death was near for her. The vision I "received" the week before was confirmed.

I had only told my mother the prior week about the

vision and so when we heard this heartbreaking news, my mother knew what was about to occur. She advised me to keep quiet of this "knowledge" I had "received" when I first told her. She just said, "pray for him", and so I did.

That week leading up to the news was very difficult for me. Knowing that someone close to him was going to die and I couldn't tell him, was weighing heavily on me. I struggled with that death "feeling" all week. When the news of her condition was told to us, the "feeling" left.

The music leader's mom died shortly after that. He never knew what I had "received" about him and reflecting back on that, my mother advised me well in not disclosing what I had "received" from God to him. I used that advice many times over since then and the uneasiness that comes with that, never changes. God have mercy!

We received a call on a Tuesday morning from the hospital from the big neighboring town that my brother was placed in an induced coma. They told us that his condition was serious and that we needed to be there as soon as possible.

My brother Juan was hospitalized in Odessa, Texas the week before with double pneumonia but he checked himself out. He worked a couple days at his job in the oil fields in West Texas and then he drove himself home to Mineral Wells for the weekend. He said he was ok and didn't need to be in the hospital. By Saturday night, his oldest daughter took him to the hospital because he was having trouble breathing. We were having dinner at one of my sister's house when we were told that my niece took him to the ER. We didn't think it was too serious. My parents went to go visit him on Sunday night and my mother said that he was still having some trouble breathing. I texted him and he said he was ok. Apparently my brother's condition was deteriorating rapidly. The decision to put him in an induced coma was made without the family's knowledge. The hospital failed to notify us of his decision. The hospital later said it was a departmental mistake on their part. That was an inexcusable mistake considering my brother's condition.

When we got the call that Tuesday morning, we all stopped what we were doing and we notified the rest of the family and relayed what was going on. Within an hour, the whole family was at the hospital.

We were all stunned by this shocking development. We all began to pray as soon as we heard the news earlier that morning. In the back of mind though, that vision of "seeing" my other brother in a coffin was starting to creep in.

We entered the ICU room where my brother was and it seemed like a bad dream. Seeing him hooked up to all those machines and tubes was heartbreaking. We immediately prayed over him asking the Lord for his healing. I brought some Lourdes Miraculous Water and a relic of Blessed Francis Xavier Seelos.

The miraculous water has been the conduit of many miracles throughout its long history dating back to 1858. The relic of Blessed Seelos has been as well. The Catholic Church in her history has venerated these relics as something very holy. Needless to say, we all prayed fervently for my brother.

The attending doctor gathered the family in a room and brought us up to date on my brother's condition. The gist of it was that he had severe sepsis and they couldn't find the source of it. His organs were taking a beating because of it. The doctor did give us hope though. There was no talk at all of this being fatal.

That night was a sleepless one for us all. We all had our phones nearby expecting news of any change in his condition. All the while, our prayers were unceasing.

The next day, I had a doctor's appointment just down the road from the hospital where he was. They discovered that I had an enlarged thyroid, which is typical for a diabetic. They scheduled an ultrasound for a later date. I really didn't put too much thought on that because of what was transpiring just down the road.

A new doctor came into the ICU that day and gave us some more information on my brother's condition. They still didn't have a solution but they did have hope that he would recover. My nephew, Juan III his oldest son, made the decision to have him transferred to a bigger and more resourceful hospital in Ft Worth, Texas.

By the time they transferred my brother, a prayer chain had already been started on social media and within many prayer circles everywhere.

The ICU and waiting room at the Ft Worth hospital, became our home for the next 48 hours. We were able to take off from work the days we were at the hospital, and we were very thankful to our employers for that.

Our parish priest Father Balaji and a visiting priest friend of his, came to the hospital prior to my brother's transfer to give him the Sacrament of Anointing of the Sick. This Sacrament took care of his soul, and now we were focusing on the healing of his body.

We prayed many Rosaries and Chaplets of Divine Mercy for my brother's soul during those long hours in the waiting room. I knew that whatever was to come, my brother's soul was healed. I don't think I've ever prayed that vigorously for anything as I did for my brother's recovery during those heart wrenching days.

As Thursday morning came, some of us who went home to try to get some rest, got the news that we needed to come to the hospital as quickly as possible as my brother Juan's condition became grave. The hope that was relayed to us just a day before was dashed. They said that he had very limited brain activity and if he did survive, that he'd mostly like be in a vegetative state. It was just a matter of time before his organs gave out. His heart was beating at an incredible rate for such a long time as well; that it was just a matter of time that he would go into cardiac arrest the doctors had said. We were still praying for a miracle.

One of the results that came from this ordeal was that some of the deep family conflicts that had been plaguing us for several years seemed to have vanished. That was one of the blessings that came out of this life-changing event. This day, which was Thursday, was grueling on us emotionally and spiritually.

Friday, October 14th is the day the De Santiago family changed forever. The morning was similar to the previous day, prayers and more prayers. The hope for a miracle was fading quickly.

The reality of that vision of death was on the forefront now. It had been since Wednesday night. Some of the family went out to eat lunch at a restaurant a few miles away when we got a text to rush back to the hospital. For a few moments during lunch, the mood seemed to be lightened just a bit. After the text, that changed.

We rushed back to the hospital and we got the news that it could be at any moment now that my brother would pass. We didn't relay this news to some of the family for obvious reasons.

My mother who has been battling depression and anxiety was struggling mightily as any mother would in this situation. Being her first born, she had a special bond with Juan. My mother was just shy of her 18th birthday when my brother was born and for a couple of years, it was just her and my brother. My father was constantly gone for work during that period and so her only solace was her first born son.

The day of my brother's passing, the Lord allowed this "Empathic Spiritual Gift" He granted me through His Spirit, to go into full gear.

The waiting room of the ICU, had other families awaiting word on their loved ones and the Lord allowed me to "feel" their passing before he allowed me to "feel" my brother's. There were two deaths before his and each time I "felt" death arrive at the moment of death.

I though it was Juan's passing each time but it wasn't. "Feeling" death on top of "feeling" their anxiousness and fear and sadness, along with those emotions of my family, really stretched my soul out. It was only by God's grace that He granted me some control during that difficult day.

We were able to have a local priest come in and pray over my brother one final time just a couple of hours before his passing. The whole family made our way to my brother's ICU room which became jammed packed with all of us in there. Some of the family stood just outside the room because there were so many of us. We held hands as the priest began his prayers. I closed my eyes and continued praying fervently for his soul. I could "feel" that Juan was ready to go. The Lord granted me that understanding during that moment of prayer. As we finished praying, one of my brothers with tears in his eyes tells me that he "felt" Juan and heard him say that he was at peace and was ready to go. He asked me if I "felt" that and I nodded my head that I did. He didn't know that I had "felt" everything the last few grueling days.

We all said our good-byes to him as we made our way back to the waiting room. I caressed my brother's temple and told him that I loved him and that we would see each other again. I told him to trust in God's infinite mercy, that he had been forgiven of all his sins. This was the last image that I wanted to keep of my brother, with all of us gathered around his bed and praying as one for his soul.

They rushed us out at that point, as my brother was beginning to go into cardiac arrest. They said that one of us could stay just outside his room as the doctors and nurses frantically began the process of resuscitating him. My nephew Juan wanted my dad or my brother Mario who had "felt" him to stay but it was decided for him to stay with his dad. I told him, "just pray" as I handed him my Rosary. He looked at me with this look that I will never forget and he said, "I'm scared". I told him, "I know, just keep praying". We made our way back to the waiting room.

The decision was made to keep resuscitating him if he went into cardiac arrest again. We wanted to give my brother Juan every chance possible to miraculously pull through but I "knew" it wasn't God's will but I prayed for that miracle anyway.

He went into cardiac arrest a couple of more times after that and my nephew Juan III, left the decision to keep resuscitating his dad up to my father. My father decided to resuscitate one more time. A couple of hours or so passed during the time of his first cardiac arrest and the last one. I was pacing up and down the long hallway just outside the waiting room praying to the Lord for His will to be done and for strength for us all. I kept rubbing on my "Jesus, I Trust in You" wristband, that I received at World Youth Day in Poland that Summer as I prayed. I called some people informing them of what was transpiring and asking them for prayers for the family. Some of my mother's friends came to be with her and support her during this unbearable day.

One of my cousins and his wife came right at this point to come and see my brother. There was no one there that was able to take them back to see him one final time and so I had to do it. The wanting of the last image of my brother that I just wrote about, was not to be. I led my cousin and his wife towards the room and I warned them how dire the situation was and how my brother was in terms of being hooked up to all the machines.

We walked in and they went to his bedside. My father, my brother, my nephew and one of my sisters were the only ones there at time. Within a few minutes it seemed like, that the final cardiac arrest began. The nurses came in quickly. My father had his hand on my brother's chest and was praying with this calmness. My nephew was kneeling by his father's right side holding his hand tightly with his head down. My sister and brother and myself stood at the foot of the bed kneeling as well praying feverishly. I had my head down praying and I glanced up a couple of times at the monitor displaying his vitals. At each glance, his vitals dropped significantly. I had my right hand on my brother's left foot as he took his final breath. One last glance at the monitor showed that he had passed from this world into the next.

I said goodbye to him one final time and I kissed him on the forehead. I volunteered to go into the waiting room and give the devastating news that Juan Estevan had just passed on this somber Friday evening. The first ones I encountered were his oldest daughter Tia and her family in the hallway. I said, "he's gone" to their painful and tear stained faces. They quickly went to his room. I then made my way into the waiting room and gave the news to the rest of the family. It was heartbreak to the most ultimate level. The rest of the family made its way to my brother's room one last time. The gut wrenching ordeal had reached its climax. I don't how else to describe what we all felt that day and the days leading up to that moment aside from life changing and heartbreaking.

Father Balaji arrived after my brother was taken away and gave us some consoling words and prayers. We are all very thankful to him and to all of those who came and supported us during that difficult time. It wasn't until the middle of the night after my brother had passed, that I shed the first tears. It all hit me at that moment. I thanked the Lord for granting us the time He gave us with my brother Juan. Our lives all changed forever that day. Little did I realize that the next several months would be numbing for me but I was consoled by my brother's "presence" on a couple of occasions to my surprise.

I believe without a doubt that the Lord had mercy on my brother. There's no question in my mind on that. It took what happened to him to save his soul. Our prayers for his conversion were answered but not like we expected. God is Mercy. For those of you praying for your "lost sheep", keep hope. The Lord will answer your prayers. We must approach His mercy with full trust. He will not abandon us, for we are His. May his mercy be glorified for all eternity!

Chapter 2: The Requiem

Making preparations for my brother Juan's funeral was surreal. The day after his death, some of us met with the funeral home to make the arrangements for his Funeral Mass and Rosary. Some music was suggested for his Mass but I quickly interjected that I was going to pick the music for the Mass. I had been listening to some Catholic musical artists for some time now and I wanted the music not to be the "standard" music that was usually chosen for funerals in our parish in Mineral Wells. I wanted the music to be uplifting and hopeful of Christ's promise of our eternal life with Him.

The Rosary for my brother was set for Monday night. Praying the Rosary on the eve of the Funeral Mass is a long-standing tradition in the Catholic Faith. It was suggested by the funeral home that one of the Church groups be in charge of it and once again I quickly interrupted telling them that the family would take lead in that as well.

It was a difficult process in setting everything up, but we made it through by God's grace. We were going to celebrate my brother's life and we weren't going to let anyone dictate to us otherwise.

As I've written in my first book, I've been granted to "see" and "experience" death by God's will. I've gone through it more times than I could count. This whole ordeal of living through the nightmare of my brother's death and arranging the funeral seemed so foreign to me but yet so familiar. How many times was I there spiritually for all those funerals for all those souls that the Lord allowed me to pray for before their deaths? Yet this feeling was perplexing to me. I didn't feel what others around me were feeling at the time. Aside from that brief breakdown the night of his passing, the reality of it all didn't hit me or perhaps, the Lord was granting me the grace of strength and courage for those that needed it around me.

After we prayed the Rosary at the funeral home and after some Scriptures were read, some of the family eulogized my brother's life. When I spoke, I spoke of God's infinite mercy and how my brother was shown great mercy at the hour of his death. "It's not the end" I said, "it's until we meet again". The Lord wept over the death of Lazarus so it was natural for us to weep for my brother Juan as well.

The Lord granted me through His Holy Spirit, the words to speak on what needed to be said at that moment. I felt the Holy Spirit guiding me.

Many people came up to me afterwards and thanked me for what I had spoken that night. Most all stopped by and gave their condolences to the family as we sat in the front pews of this funeral home chapel.

They all came up with tears in their eyes as came up one by one. It was a steady stream of people and my thought was "they are all sadder that I am about this". Like I said before it was all God's doing. It would all hit me a little later down the line though.

One of the supernatural occurrences that was confirmed

right before we left the funeral home that night, came from one of my cousins.

My cousin came up to me and recounted that while she couldn't go to the hospital to see Juan, she "received" a vision of the Virgin Mary under her title of Our Lady of Lourdes. In the vision, Our Lady came and met my brother upon his passing and led him to Our Lord in Heaven. I was happily surprised by that because one of my nieces, Marina, whom I wrote about in the first book about the Virgin Mary dream, recounted the exact same vision at the hospital when Juan passed away. I called Marina over and told her to recount her vision to my cousin. My cousin had this big smile on her face knowing that the vision she "received" was truly from Heaven.

That vision gave us all comfort. I knew Our Lady was there with my brother the moment he died, because I also "saw" her there that day. The Lord in His loving mercy allowed us to "receive" this spiritual consolation in this trying time for our family.

The Funeral Mass, which I thought was going to be difficult spiritually for me because of the "empathic gift", wasn't. There was an abundance of sadness but the Lord blocked out most of the emotions there, which would've typically bombarded me. Thank you Lord for that grace.

The Church was packed, that was a testament to my brother's generous heart. My brother was loved by so many people and that made my heart happy. We all mourned in our own way with his passing. It all came to a head shortly after for me as I struggled with my health. Anxiety attacks came at a fever pitch in the months afterwards but I offered that entire struggle up for the conversion of souls. I even had a trip to the ER because of it. I was overloaded with this "Empathic Spiritual Gift" and it took a toll on me.

The one thing that I didn't mention to anyone is that I "felt" Juan's presence there at the Funeral Mass. I "know" he was there because I was given to "feel" him as well. This wasn't a rare occasion in terms of "feeling" departed souls at funerals. There were many more before this solemn day.

Chapter 3: The Faithful Departed

The first funeral I remember going to was that of my 15-year-old cousin who passed away as the result of a car accident. I don't remember much detail about it though, as I was only 7 years old at the time.

The next funeral I do remember clearly. It was of my great-grandmother on my mom's side of the family. My parents and I traveled to Mexico for her funeral. I had just started middle school and I was a little older and so my memory is clearer on the details.

I remember it being very warm in this very small funeral home. They had like a clear plastic hard cover over her top part of her body as she lay in her coffin. It reminded me of a Barbie doll in its packaging. Her family was pressing down on the cover crying very loudly. I could see the handprints all over the plastic from where I was sitting. I had no feeling over this death. I only felt a little fear because of the loud wailing coming from one of the women there crying over my great-grandmother's body.

Some aunts and uncles have passed away, as well as both my grandmothers, during the period from my great-grandmothers death until my "life" as I call it began.

The first time I stepped into a funeral home when this "new world" was opened to me, was an overwhelming feeling.

We were called on a regular basis to clean the carpet of the funeral home that is right across the street from our Church in my hometown. As soon as I stepped into the main viewing room, I "felt" what seemed like all the sadness that had accumulated in there over the years. I felt heavy. I would close my eyes and "see" the countless people shedding tears over their loved ones. I had to walk out of there because it was too much for me to handle. As soon as I would walk back into that area, the feeling came back. I only "felt" that the first time we cleaned there when this "life" started. We went back many times since to clean and I never "felt" that feeling again. I believe it was because the Lord had granted me spiritual maturity and the grace to block out things like this because situations like these were overwhelming in the early years.

As I wrote in the last chapter, the grace of "feeling" the faithful departed began early in this journey of mine.

The Rosary, on the eve of the funeral of an older parishioner who attended daily Mass with us, is when I was first granted this particular grace.

In the chapel/viewing area where I first "felt" the overwhelming sadness when I was working, is when this grace occurred. The Rosary was about halfway done when I "heard" this sweet old lady speak. At first I didn't know what I was hearing. I then quickly realized I was "hearing" this older lady speak. I rebuked it because it surprised me. I didn't think it was from God at that point because the thought of seeing people "talking" to the dead on TV came to mind. I know the Catholic Church forbids those types of things such as divinity, seances and things of that nature. In reading about the Saints though, I know that some of them encountered souls who had passed on. It was always for a purpose. It was usually for a message or to have prayers said on their behalf and so I know there was plenty of precedence on this. I prayed for discernment on all this to be sure it was from the Lord. I'm very conscious of the Church's teachings on the supernatural and I pray that the Holy Spirit never allows me to stray from Her teachings.

This soul was "telling" me tell to her family that she loved them and everything was going to be ok. I didn't say anything of course because I didn't know if it was from God or not. I didn't realize until the next time this occurrence happened, that this truly was of God and He was allowing it to happen.

It was strange "hearing" this while seeing everyone there mourning and paying their respect to this pious woman. I was siting there thinking, "is anyone else hearing this?".

This was a death that I was given to "see" and pray for beforehand. Perhaps it was one of the reasons I was granted that grace during her Rosary.

When I relayed this "knowledge" that I was given about this death to someone close to this woman, I didn't realize that I came off without any sensitivity to the person's grief.

The Lord more than made up for it for me, when He allowed me to "see" how this pious woman was greeted as she entered Eternity. She was greeted by the embrace of the Holy Virgin Mary who then led her to her son Our Lord Jesus. I "saw" this vision very clearly. As I told this account to the grieving friend, the Holy Spirit filled me up with this incredible sensation of confirmation that was out of this world. My whole body was electric! It was an incredible privilege to be able to "see" that greeting of this soul in Heaven! Praise Be to God!

The next occurrence of this phenomenon happened a couple of years later after this one, I "knew" it was from Above immediately. It was late Summer of 2014 when this funeral took place and again I was given to "see" this death before it occurred. I was given to "see" this in a dream months before it happened. When I "received" this death, the man was healthy. Shortly after, he got very sick and battled this cancer for a short time before he passed. I prayed for his soul many times before he passed.

Images of the vision became reality as I sat in our Church while attending his funeral. During the Funeral Mass, I "heard" this departed soul speak. It was a message to his grieving wife. He said to tell his wife not to worry, for her not to pray to see him one more time because if she could see what he was seeing at that moment, she wouldn't want to take him away from that. I wasn't "shown" what he was seeing. It was obvious to me that it was Heaven and it felt like I wasn't supposed to have a glimpse of it. I was given just enough to "feel" the smallest possible fraction of it to know what it was on the "other side".

I wanted to tell this grieving widow this message but I kept going back and forth in my mind if I should or not. I wanted to, I really did but eventually I didn't. She was so grief stricken, that it would've sent her into a more grief stricken state if I would've told her right after the funeral. She knew my family for a long time and I only had brief contact with her up to that point. She didn't know anything about my "life" and so that added more to the "don't tell her" side.

I hope and pray that it was the Holy Spirit that prevented me from passing along that message. I feel as time has gone by, that the message will be given to her in time. It's all in God's timing.

Another funeral that happened not too long after that, the same thing took place. The deceased was an older woman who passed away after a long battle with cancer. She wanted the message that she will be watching over her husband to be passed along. I didn't say anything in that situation either. I could "see" her watching over him already.

People who have limited knowledge of the supernatural have a strong tendency to question things of this nature. After what I went through in 2010 as I wrote about in my first book about the unbelievers and naysayers, it made me hesitant to pass along messages to people.

I did pass along a message a little later that year to someone whom I traveled with during my first pilgrimage to Italy. This young woman's father had passed away some years earlier. I gave the message and she fully believed it. It confirmed to her what she had been believing all along. The message was meant for her and so I will not relay it here. This young woman knew a little about this "life" of mine through several conversations I had with her after our pilgrimage back in 2013.

The most powerful of these encounters though was that of my brother Juan.

In 2017, several months after his passing, I could "feel" his presence with me. The Lord grants me this "knowledge" of what I'm "feeling". In my brother's case, I could "see" him in a constant vision. I would close my eyes and I "see" him in my mind's eye. It's similar to how I'm given to "see" certain people when I'm "feeling "their soul conditions or when I "know" that a certain vision is about someone.

The presence of my brother had the same feel as when I'm given to "feel" Heavenly presences. I could sense he was watching over me. This happened on a couple of occasions.

The strongest one occurred when I was working. I was praying as do while I work and I came to the realization that I could ask my brother for his intercession as we believe that we can do with the Heavenly Saints.

My brother is with our Lord and so that makes him a Saint. He's not canonized by the Church as so, but anyone in Heaven is technically a Saint. I start praying, asking for his intercession for my family especially for my mother and for his children. I asked for some personal intentions I had as well. The intercessions lasted about 10 minutes or so. I began to "feel" his presence like how I just described but it was more intense. His presence was strong. I thanked him and I said, "that's enough of my asking for things from you.

Thank you my brother. I love you!". At that moment, I "felt" his strong presence leave me. That Heavenly presence was gone and it felt normal again. I teared up with this incredible grace I had just received from the Lord. It gave me some consolation because his loss has been hard on the family. I know he prays for us and watches over us as well.

The last occurrence in which I will talk about happened during my time in prayer group. This time it was an apparition with no words but with an infused understanding of the message, This was from a 7 year-old boy named Bobby.

Chapter 4: Bobby

I first saw Bobby at the Charismatic Prayer Meeting I attended from 2006-2010. Bobby, who was 7 years old at time, came with his mother to one of our meetings. I'm assuming they were there because of an invite from one of the families that regularly attending these very prayerful gatherings.

I didn't really pay much attention to Bobby and his mother at first, because we usually had visitors who came to our weekly Thursday meetings and secondly, because of my early struggles with the supernatural.

It was around halfway through our 2 hour plus meeting, when I saw Bobby run across our large circular seating arrangement and run into the arms of one of our long time members.

It was at that moment that I received a very powerful vision. It was as though I was transported to another time and place.

I saw myself in the huge grassy field and as I began observing my surroundings, this green open-ended tent appeared along with many grave markers. I quickly realize that I was at the cemetery that sits just south of my small town of Mineral Wells. I then see the same long time member who Bobby ran to just seconds before, sitting in the front row of folded chairs in front of a coffin. It was a funeral that was taking place. I see this very grim look on this member's face as I intently look at him. I was trying to see whose funeral it was but I couldn't see from my vantage point. As fast as I was transported into this vision at the cemetery, I was quickly returned just as fast. I found myself back in the Church hall where we always met for our meetings. I began to try to discern what it was I just "saw". I prayed hard, asking the Lord the meaning of this vision. I received my answer a couple of weeks later.

A couple of weeks later, the prayer group received the news that Bobby was diagnosed with an aggressive brain tumor. He was having symptoms typically associated with a brain tumor when his mother took him to the doctor. This diagnosis was a shock to his family, as it would be to any family.

As soon as I heard this news, I reverted back to what I was given a couple of weeks earlier with the vision that started the moment Bobby ran into the arms of this prayer group member. Was this vision the impending death of Bobby? I rebuked it immediately.

During the subsequent weeks at our meetings, Bobby and his mother became regulars. We prayed unceasingly for Bobby's healing. Many members laid hands and prayed over him with great fervor. All the while, this apparent vision of death was weighing on me. I didn't tell anyone of course. Everyone had hope that the Lord was going to heal him through our collective prayers. I wasn't going to go against that hope. I was hoping I was wrong in my discernment of this vision but I knew in my heart I wasn't.

As Bobby's condition began to worsen, an emergency Baptism was organized. The Baptism took place instead of our prayer meeting. The Chapel was packed and our young priest at the time administered the Sacrament to Bobby. All of Bobby's family and extended family was there. The mood of all the people in attendance were of hope and optimism except for my demeanor. All I "felt" was death. Nobody thought death was on the horizon despite Bobby's condition worsening. The "feeling" for me was getting stronger. The Baptism felt like a funeral to me. It all "felt" so dark to me. I had to contain my emotions amongst all these people.

We all then went to the Church hall as a huge meal was prepared for everyone in celebration of the Baptism.

After the meal, the prayer group wanted to pray for this young boy once more. The long time members of the group including my parents and myself, were part of the group praying over him. I positioned myself right in front of Bobby as we prayed. I was hoping that the Lord would grant me another vision of Bobby as we were all praying. I was hoping He would "show" me his healing or that I discerned this death vision wrong. I prayed hard but I didn't "receive" anything.

Bobby and his mother continued coming to the prayer meetings after that until Bobby couldn't go out anymore. Some people from the group would go over to his house and visit him but I never went. I don't know why I didn't; maybe it was because I "knew" what was coming.

We inevitably received the news that Bobby had passed away. Everyone was distraught. Questions of why the Lord didn't heal him crossed a lot of people's mind. I knew otherwise. I "knew" the vision that I "received" that fateful day would unfold despite our best intentions.

God's plan for us is a mystery at times. We don't know why things like this happen but we trust in Him, trust in His Divine will.

The images of that vision came to pass, as the person, who Bobby ran to, was front and center during the Funeral Mass and burial as in the vision.

The funeral for me felt like what most of the people were feeling during his Baptism, hope and joy. The mourning Church said otherwise but the Lord allowed me to "see" and "know" that Bobby was with Him in Paradise.

The incredible grace to "see" Bobby after his passing to deliver a message, as I had with others, came not to long after his death.

His mother continued to come to the weekly meetings to seek solace of the passing of her young child. This one particular Thursday, as we prayed for her, I "received" an apparition of the young boy. I "saw" him standing there looking at me. He appeared to me wearing some dress pants and a long sleeved shirt and tie. He had this incredible smile on his face. I "received" this infused message that I was to tell his mother that he was with the Lord and was happy and that he was the Lord's "little angel" now. This vision was confirmed by another person in the group who "felt" his presence there and but saw only his smile.

I passed along the message without hesitation to his

mother as we continued praying for her. I told her as I got closer to her, what I had "received". She began crying and I believe she received some of the solace she was desperately searching for.

The pain she had was tremendous. I delivered another message to her some time after that. I believe that private message was a part of the Lord's continued healing of this grieving mother.

That message came at the time when I was delivering messages at an unbelievable rate as I wrote about in my first book. I remember giving Bobby's aunt who was also there, a message, which surprised her because it was something that only she knew it to be true. That was just more confirmation of what I "receiving", was in fact from the Lord.

This "knowledge" became a regular occurrence ever since this journey of mine began back in 2006.

Chapter: 5 "Knowledge"

The Charism of "The Word of Knowledge", is a supernatural revelation of facts past, present or future which we did not learn through the efforts of the natural mind. This is not to be confused with the knowledge we have acquired through the study of Scriptures.

This "knowledge" began very early in my conversion in 2006. From the beginning, I would "receive" things from Above with no explanation of how or why I knew certain things about people and situations and so forth.

Like I mentioned in my first book, I would "know" if people had died in the house where we would go and do work at through our carpet cleaning service. I just knew things. It was like an infused knowledge. Often times I felt a disturbance in my soul or something would trigger the infusion of this knowledge.

One of the early examples of this took place within a month and half of my first vision. My family and I were doing a job during our weekly work routine when this disturbance hit my soul. I felt real uneasy as I usually do when these supernatural occurrences strike me. My soul became pained with this hurt, and the peace I was carrying was quickly removed to make room for this grace from God. I prayed to "receive" the reasoning for this disturbance and I quickly "received" my answer.

I "saw" one of my brothers in this vision. I told one of my sisters who was working with me what I had just "received". I told her that I "saw" our 2nd oldest brother and I gave her this explanation as of why. I told her without even thinking, that someone was planning to file a lawsuit against him. I don't know where that thought came from or how it even formed in my thoughts, but I blurted this out to her. I offered some prayers for my brother as I typically do when I "receive" things of this supernatural origin from Our Lord through His Holy Spirit.

About a week later, my brother calls us and tells us that someone had just filed a lawsuit against him. We were surprised that what I had "received" just a week before, came to pass. To me, this was just more confirmation from Our Lord that He had fully entered my life and had begun working in me in this supernatural way. I admit that this revelation was a relief in terms that I wasn't delusional or that I had some mental deficiencies. So much was coming in terms of revelations that it didn't seem to be possible for these things to be happening to me. I knew that these things happened to the Holy Saints of the Church but who was I to "receive" such things.

I was a little afraid when these revelations started to come to pass with frequency. Why was the Lord allowing me to "know" so much? Why was He asking this of me? These questions ran through my mind quite a bit in those early years.

When I would give testimony to God working in my life in this way, people would comment on how they would love to have this "Gift of Knowledge". To them, this supernatural gift and others that the Holy Spirit had granted me, seemed like superpowers that one gets fascinated with through movies and television shows that dominates our pop culture today. I explain to them that these "gifts" are not "superpowers", that they are not to be regarded lightly.

I understand their fascination as I was once thought like them. I use to daydream quite frequently about having "superpowers", specifically "knowing" things before they would happen and of also having telekinesis, the ability to move things with my mind.

Even on this journey that the Lord has me on, I have had countless dreams of having telekinesis. I'm not 100% sure of why these dreams are still occurring. Perhaps it's just old memories that are still in my subconscious and are resurfacing on occasion.

There's one incident that happened a couple of years before this conversion of mine started, that sticks out in particular. Perhaps that incident fueled those dreams.

I was driving back from Ft Worth, Texas and traveling westbound back to my hometown of Mineral Wells. I was about 15 miles west of Ft Worth traveling on the highway in the middle lane. Traffic was somewhat light and I was just behind this truck pulling a flatbed utility trailer that is pretty common in Texas. The truck was in the lane to my right. I was probably in that position for a couple of minutes when I started to fixate my gaze on the trailer. The thought of "what if the back left wheel comes off" ran through my mind. I began to drive more cautiously as this became more than a thought. In that moment the back left wheel came off the trailer and bounced a few times before it hit a car in the eastbound lanes. Being prepared by the "thought", I was able to avoid this dangerous bouncing wheel.

I was shocked that this "thought" became a reality. Was this a precursor to the "Gift of Knowledge" that lay dormant at the point in my life? I told this story to one of my Confirmation classes and one of my students commented that it was a superpower, specifically telekinesis. I just laughed a bit and said no. My former self would've probably agreed with him to a degree.

This "knowledge" has extended to other areas, to random things. We've all had those moments when something had to come pass and we've said, "I knew that was going to happen!". This "knowledge" for me in these random situations, have been more of infused understanding of what was coming. It's particularly striking in watching sporting events. Perhaps it's because I'm focusing on the action of the sport I'm watching that this "gift" comes into play. I admit that in situations like this, I get a little smile on my face knowing that the Spirit of God works in every facet of my life even in trivial things like sporting events.

There have been some situations throughout my journey that this gift has gone very deep in terms of "knowing" things.

In late 2006 just a few months into my conversion, there was a particular woman who had been given some very erroneous information about me and to that effect spoke ill of me to others. She was a worker in this big superstore in my small hometown in which I frequented. This particular Autumn day, she walks right past me as I was making my way to go get something to eat in this built-in fast food place in this huge superstore. The moment we passed each other, her thoughts about me rang loudly in my head. It was as though she had spoken these unkind thoughts to me out loud. It was in an instant that this "knowledge" occurred. This woman didn't even acknowledge me as she passed me. I didn't know how to react to this. I was thrown off with the fact that I "heard" her, and with the realization of the unpleasantness of her words towards me. I continued on towards ordering my food and I greeted the fast food worker as I usually do. With this experience still with me, I asked the worker if she had ever felt that someone didn't like her while being in the same area as that person. The kind worker said "yes", that she did feel when someone didn't care for her. I replied if she ever felt that feeling even deeper like knowing their ill intent, knowing exactly what they truly were thinking. With her raised eyebrows, she had this surprised look on face and answered, "no, never that deep". At that moment the realization that this woman whose thoughts I was given to "hear", offended me quite deeply. I went from amazement to angry in an instant. "How dare she speak this malice towards me, she doesn't even know me", ran through my head as I was paying for my order. I then decided to go confront this woman but I stopped myself before I even took a step. How could I confront her? What was I going say? I couldn't tell her that I "heard" her thoughts about me. She probably would've thought I was crazy or something. I thank the Lord I didn't say anything to her. I don't think I ever saw that woman again after that. I believe she left her job shortly after that.

There was another incident a few years after this that I had to hold my tongue when this "knowledge" occurred again.

In early 2010, I went with my parents and some family friends to a weekend Charismatic Renewal Workshop in Ft. Worth, TX.

The day began with Mass and with some Praise and Worship before the workshop itself began. This took place at a Catholic High School. We gathered in the school library to begin the workshop that was going to be given by a priest the organizers had brought in from out of state. My parents and I sat in the chairs that were set up for the attendees. We noticed that the 2 women, the family friends, weren't there. We went to the hallway just outside the library to see what was going on. One of our friends was being told by one of organizers, that she couldn't stay for this particular workshop. This woman told our friend that the workshop was too advanced for her and that she didn't attended a previous workshop which also prohibited her from attending this one. While listening to this woman explaining all this, I was given to "know" her evil intent. She was thinking very ill of our friend, and was purposely making these "restrictions" because of a previous dispute she had with her. She was getting joy in telling her she couldn't attend even though her face didn't show it. I got angry because I was "shown" all this and I was on the verge of interrupting and calling her out on this right in front of a lot people. Once again, the Lord held my tongue. I knew it would've caused a scene had I said something in anger. Our friends decided to leave the workshop and head back home. I decided to go back with them. I didn't want to be a part of something that this malicious woman was involved with. My parents stayed behind though because my mom told this woman that her and my dad weren't leaving. My mom told her that we had made a big sacrifice in coming there and so they stayed. My mom was upset with this woman as well. While driving back with our 2 other friends, we discussed what had just transpired. I didn't reveal to them what the Lord had "given" me. I felt it wasn't the proper time.

We arrived at the house of one of our friends after we had lunch. We continued talking about what had occurred earlier. I don't recall the exact situation but I "knew" something occurred after we left the workshop that rang a bell. I quickly grabbed my backpack and I took out my journal and looked back on a dream I had a few days earlier that I had written down. It was exactly what had happened after we left. I showed the 2 ladies what I had written. They were surprised. I said that we weren't meant to stay at the workshop, hence the prophetic dream. Had we stayed, the dream wouldn't of come to pass. My question though, was that truly the case? Was this dream part of "Gift of Prophecy" I had received? Did the events have to transpire as such in order for the dream to come to pass? As I've written before, the Lord has "shown" me things via dreams that had no rhyme or reason to them but were prophetic in nature because they came to pass. Only the Lord knows the answers to these questions.

There have been many more occasions where I've been given to "know" people's thoughts. It occurred a lot more in the early years of my conversion than they do now. It still happens on occasion but I have more of a block, a shield up against that and with a lot of other things. When that shield is down I "hear", "feel", and "sense" everything.

I'm grateful that the Lord has granted me that protection because it gets pretty intense when this protective shield comes down.

On Holy Thursday in 2017, the Lord allowed the shield to come down in a big way.

After my brother passed in late 2016, I didn't "receive" much in terms of being "given" things from Above to pray for. I dealt with my many personal struggles up to that Holy Thursday. It overwhelmed me to say the least.

That Thursday my Confirmation class that I teach had to participate in the Holy Thursday Mass.

It started with my blood sugar falling. I "felt" something along with that. I ate some cookies in the Church kitchen to deal with the low blood sugar. I "felt" pain and sadness at that moment which wasn't mine. I began to tear up. This sudden pain hurt deeply. My friend came to check up on me to see if I was ok. I told her that I wasn't. Mass had started and I made my way inside the Church and I sat in the very back pew. My Confirmation class sat in the front and I was in no condition to sit amongst them. My blood sugar had gone up to a steady normal level but these "feelings" I had increased.

I started to "feel" everyone in the Church at that moment. I "felt" the good and the bad. I couldn't control it. I "sensed" everything there. The floodgates of the "supernatural gifts" that I had "received" many years earlier came back in a rush at that moment. It overwhelmed me.

The weekend before, I started "sensing" something as I prayed in the Chapel. I started crying for no reason. I believe it was the Lord preparing to restart His purpose for me. I believe He gave me a break for a few months after my brother's passing to deal with it. It was time to restart and I needed to be ready.

Ironically just a couple of years earlier on a Holy Thursday, I received from Our Lord that my journey He had me on was about to get a little more intense.

Chapter 6: "Heal My People"

On Holy Thursday 2014, the Confirmation Class was in charge of the first hour of Adoration after Mass. We processed from the big Church into the Chapel when Mass had ended. We had some Scriptures passages to be read by some of the Confirmation candidates in-between some music I had picked out. I was preoccupied with being sure we had everything in order but it all went well. When our hour ended, the next Church group began their hour in leading the parishioners in Adoration. I was then able to relax with my duties finished. At that point, I began to fervently pray while adoring Our Lord.

I'm not sure how long into prayer I was when I "sensed" something. The praise and worship music I had played earlier was still playing for the next group, and so I was enveloped in the Spirit. I then heard the words from Our Lord, "do you love Me?" and I replied, "yes Lord I love you". Then the Lord said, "heal My people". A second time, "do you love Me?" and I said again, "Yes Lord I love You". By this time, tears were running down my cheeks at a steady pace. Then finally like St Peter's exchange with Our Lord when He asked Peter the same thing after the Resurrection, "do you Love Me?" and I said once again, "yes Lord I do!" and then a final time Our Blessed Lord said, "heal My people". I was trying to contain my crying so as not to attract attention at that point. I didn't fully understand why that exchange with the Lord occurred at that moment. I was overwhelmed with what He was asking of me. Needless to say, I spent a lot of time discerning exactly how He wanted this done.

As I wrote in the first book on my experience with praying over people and the "laying of hands", this was nothing new to me, but this "command" of Our Lord was.

In the first book I wrote about several instances of people receiving healing from the Lord after I was "given" the grace to pray for them. It was part of what we did in the Prayer Group, praying over people. There were many dreams in the early years of people needing physical healing and by the "gift of healing" from the Holy Spirit, I was able to "lay hands" on them and they would be healed. I always knew that it was something that I was given from Above but now, this was full on confirmation from Jesus Himself.

There was a second call from Our Lord after that Holy Thursday a couple months later, asking for healing once again. This call came via a dream.

In the dream, I was in my hometown Chapel but it looked a little different. The altar was facing in a different direction. I see our former priest who passed away a few years ago walking around the altar. I'm somewhere near the front of the Chapel just standing there and then I hear a loud voice come out of nowhere, "heal so you can heal" and with that I woke up. I woke with the incredible sense that the voice was that of Our Lord. "Heal so you can heal", "what does that mean?" I thought to myself. I knew it was connected to the exchange from Holy Thursday. Did the Lord mean that I needed to be healed so I could "heal

His people"? Was it that I needed to "heal" others by the "gift of healing" so I could receive my healing? I had been praying for healing almost daily since I was diagnosed with Type 1 Diabetes in early 2010 and I didn't know if my healing was in reference to that.

The third call for healing came about a month later. It was a Monday I believe and I was "feeling" something. I prayed on this "feeling" but it lingered as the day went on. I know I was going through a rough stretch of "receiving" from Above because I was mentally and spiritually drained quite a bit leading up to this day. The "feeling" of this day reached its peak by the late evening. I texted a friend and we ended up talking on the phone, as she was a little concerned on how I was feeling. I explained how I was drained with everything that I was "receiving" during that time and also with this new "feeling" I had that day. I told her that it was extremely difficult to discern what this "feeling" was in this state. She went to go get her "Daily Devotional" book as we continued talking. This book had daily Scriptural passages and spiritual help.

She read that day's passages and it ended up being exactly what I needed. It described what I was going through, what I had just explained to her. The core of the message was that I needed to quiet my soul so I could "hear" what the Lord was telling me. I was like "wow!" the Lord saw my struggle and used my friend to help me. We were both amazed at the incredible way the Lord worked that night. I thanked her for her help and I hung the phone and tried to quiet my soul. I sat in the living room on this big leather sectional couch in the dark. I prayed asking the Holy Spirit to calm the "noise". Being late at this point, I began dozing off and

I entered this state which I will explain more on in a later chapter, that's in-between being awake and being asleep. I "received" a vision. I don't remember what exactly I "saw" but what I "heard" was loud and clear. This voice was similar to the one from the dream in the second calling that occurred a month earlier.

This resounding voice said, "you've been given the power to heal", and with that I was fully awake. The long drawn out "feeling" from this day was immediately gone.

I realized the Lord was trying to give me this message all day but I was too engrossed in the "noise" to listen. He had to use my friend to shut me up so I could "hear".

Three callings in 4 months. The Lord was unmistakingly calling me to a new ministry. The question I was asking the Lord now was," how am I supposed to do this?".

I spent a lot of time discerning this new call to healing. I've have been a part of many instances of healing as I mentioned earlier but this "heal so I can heal" was something of a twist.

I never stopped believing that my disease, the Type 1 diabetes, was going to be temporary. I began to assume that the "heal so I can heal" was referring to my illness and my personal healing.

Ever since my diagnosis I've prayed to be healed pretty much on a daily basis. I received the Sacrament of the Anointing of the Sick a few times and I attended many healing Masses as well, but the healing never came. So was this instruction from Our Lord finally signaling my healing of this awful disease?

In September of 2010, my parents and I and some friends of ours, attending a weekend Charismatic Renewal conference in Allen, TX. Allen, TX is just outside of Dallas. We made this 2-hour drive early on a Saturday morning. One of the reasons I wanted to go was that a speaker, who had been given the "gift healing", was going to be there. Being just 6 months into discovering I had this disease, I was eager to go as I thought I had carried this disease long enough. I figured it was time to be healed by the Lord.

The conference was very powerful and moving that first day. The presence of the Lord and His Spirit was very evident. The day's events ended with healing prayers and Adoration. The speaker, the one with the healing gift, began his prayers with the Blessed Lord ever present in the Holy Eucharist in this large golden Monstrance that was brought out to this makeshift altar. The packed sports arena's lights were dimmed and the praise and worship music was very moving, setting up the environment for "healing" to take place.

My parents and I were in the stands for the first part of the conference, while the altar and the guest speakers were on the floor level of the arena.

When the Adoration and healing prayers began, my mother and I made our way to the floor level. It was very crowded on the floor level and so we stood on the opposite side of the altar where it was a little less congested. My mother and I were praying fervently for my healing at that point. The speaker, while praying for healing, would say something like, "there is a person here suffering from" and then he would mention an illness. He continued by saying that a particular person or persons with that affliction, was healed by the Lord. I could hear crying all around me. I was praying that the speaker would somehow call my disease and me. Finally he says, "there are 2 people in the back who are suffering from Diabetes, the Lord has healed you!". My mother and I looked at each other. We felt that I was one of the 2 since we were in the back on the floor level. We quickly made our way closer to the altar and I was very emotional at this point. I was crying giving thanks to the Lord for this healing. I cried for a while because even though I was only 6 months into this diagnosis, I was tired of having this illness and I was relieved that it was gone, or at least I believed it was.

We had dinner afterwards and I was trying to process what had just occurred. Was I truly healed? I checked my blood sugar just once a day at that point and only in the mornings, which was very ignorant of me. I was very uneducated as a diabetic in that first year. I didn't know what my blood sugar was until the next morning when I woke up. When I checked it the next day it was high. I was told and I had read that sometimes healings are gradual and so I thought at that point that my healing had to be gradual. I cautiously ate very unhealthy that day as we went home on Sunday. The next 2 mornings, my blood sugar readings were lower and lower than the previous day. I thought, "the healing is happening!". The third morning my blood sugar shot way up. The subsequent mornings as well. What happened? Was I not healed?

My health severely declined over the next 6 months. I

was put on insulin and got a crash course in diabetes management. As I was getting sicker and sicker, I refused to go on insulin because I thought, "I was healed at the conference and I have to believe that I was". I thought I was being tested by the Lord and if I went on insulin, that meant I failed His test. I got so sick that I finally relented and was put on a regular insulin regiment. I felt better after a few weeks of being on insulin. My health dramatically improved. Someone said to me that perhaps the healing I "received" was in the form of insulin. My health improving as it did was the proof they said. I didn't buy it.

As I further discerned these callings from the Lord, I was led to read some books on healing. One in particular was from Dr. Frances Macnutt, a former priest. His book "Healing" was very insightful. Dr. Macnutt wrote that at times physical healing is linked to spiritual healing. We needed to look back on our lives to see where and if this spiritual, interior healing was needed. I was able to make a good confession after I had an extensive look back on my life. I believe my call to heal needed to begin interiorly. It's a process that's still going on and by God's grace, I will be completely healed spiritual and interior wise.

As Dr. Macnutt explained in his book, to be an instrument of the Lord in this capacity, we need to diagnose the person in whom we are praying for to see what type of healing is needed. The Holy Spirit guides us in this discernment. There is much more than just "laying hands" and praying for healing that I came to find out through the various books the Lord led me too. These 3 callings were just the beginning. I needed to be prepared in order to carry out this mission and these books put me on that path.

I prayed with this renewed fervor for my healing. I believed that my praying for myself would result in my healing. There were many occasions when I would pray for myself when I had illnesses, that these infirmities were healed immediately.

On some of those occasions, I had prayed with a great intent because I had obligations that I couldn't miss and I couldn't afford to be sick.

One of those occasions occurred during my last pilgrimage to Lourdes in October of 2017. About half of my family went to France and Italy that Fall. We wanted to be in a special place to commemorate the 1st anniversary of my brother Juan's passing and so we chose Lourdes, France.

We had to spend the first night of our trip in Paris before we left to Lourdes early the next morning. After dinner, I began to feel sick immediately. I felt nauseous. Around midnight, I got up multiple times to throw up. I ended up throwing up 6 times, which I had never done so much in my entire life that I can recall. Then the bowel issues started. One of my brothers who was staying with me in this hotel room was up as well. I felt bad that my sickness kept him up. I had given up hope that I was going to make the flight the next morning to Lourdes. I imagined myself being stuck in the hotel alone for the next few days while the rest of the family was in Lourdes. I finally laid down halfway on my bed with my hand on my stomach praying for a miraculous healing. I fell asleep and I awoke a few hours later completely healed. I was surprised to be honest. I was a little tired but I was able to eat breakfast at the airport with no ill effects. There were no signs of illness that plagued me just hours earlier. We all got on a plane to Lourdes and had an incredible and grace filled trip. I know the Blessed Mother had her hand in this healing as well.

In the middle of 2017, the sense that I needed to do something in regards to this new mission was as strong as ever. I prayed for more confirmation and the Blessed Lord delivered.

One of those confirmations came at morning Mass. After an intense prayer for confirmation the night before, the homily by our priest Father Balaji the next morning began with "you are called to be healers". I lit up at that moment realizing that the Lord was truly calling me to this healing ministry. Like with most things I "receive" though, I kept seeking confirmation.

Days after this Mass, I was texting a friend about some spiritual matters and she responds to one my texts with "so you can heal people?". I wasn't talking about that specifically but she replied with that. I asked her why she responded that way and she said it just seemed like that's what I needed to do. I was once again answered by the Lord.

Like I've written before, there have been many occasions where I've "laid hands" on people and they received healing or immediate relief of their pains. I know there have been moments where there were no doubts in my mind that I needed to pray for someone and it was going to result in healing. One of those moments came on a Saturday night about 7 or 8 years ago. Two of my nephews, who are brothers, were over spending the night at the house. They were around 10 and 7 years old at the time. They were both sick and my mother asked me to pray for them. The 10-year-old looked at me with some doubt as I placed my hand on his head and began to pray for healing. He had been sick for a day or two when I prayed over him. I told him after I prayed for him that he was gonna to wake up the next morning completely healed. The next morning, he was. There was no sign of the sickness.

Some would say that wouldn't constitute a true healing because perhaps his illness was at its end and a good night's rest played a part in his waking up 100% better. I could see that but in this case, his little brother who was also sick from a different illness at the same time was healed after I prayed over him. My little nephew was in so much pain in his legs that the medicine he took for it made him sleep. I "knew" that after the prayers of healing that he was going to be free from the extreme pain that he was crying from just hours earlier. He woke up with no signs of the pain. The next day he was running around like a normal 7-year-old. I just smiled at the incredible power of God's mercy and love. Those little boys didn't know what a beautiful grace they received at the time but I knew. The Divine Healer healed them!

Finally after a very strong prompting of the Holy Spirit, I went to speak with Father Balaji on a hot muggy Sunday afternoon in July of 2017. I was speaking to a friend at the Church when this prompting peaked. She encouraged me to act on it and so I did.

Father Balaji and I went into the Chapel and I began to

explain to him the 3 callings. He had been familiar with some of the other things I had "received" and so this wasn't something that was a surprise to him. He was very supportive. There was no doubt in his mind that the Lord was calling me to this mission. He said that people would be more receptive to me if I were a priest or even a deacon. I told him that I didn't having a calling for that. I prayed and discerned that for a while and I know that's not the path the Lord was calling me to.

He said that we had to be careful on how we needed to proceed with this because Catholics in the West aren't generally familiar with these types of Charisms as they are in India. In the Charismatic Renewal though, it's a different story. It's common knowledge that healing takes place on a regular basis.

Father said I could pray some prayers of healing at the end of our First Friday Adorations every month but not do the "laying of hands". The next First Friday was less than a week away and I was excited.

I told Father of a dream I had just the week before. In the dream, Father and I were in front of the altar and we were praying for healing. There were 2 lines of people, one line for Father and one line for me. We would each "lay hands" on the people and prayed as they came up. In my line, a young woman that I know from our parish came up and I prayed for her. She then went back to her pew and sat with her mother. I see that she had no reaction to my prayers and so I followed her back to her pew. She was now laying her head on her mother's lap. She looks at me and said that she needed prayers for her stomach and so I placed my hands on her stomach and prayed for healing. I then woke up at that point. The next morning I messaged the young woman and told her about the dream. She replied, " I didn't tell you about my stomach problems?" I said "no". She then proceeded to tell me that she's had issues for a while with her stomach and sometimes she goes some days without eating because of it. She thought the dream was a neat coincidence. It didn't occur to her that it was something from Above.

Another parishioner also relayed a dream to me in which Father Balaji and I were in front of the main Church's altar praying for people. This was relayed to me after the meeting I had with Father. This was just further confirmation on what the Lord wanted me to do.

The First Friday came and I was nervous. I spent quite a bit of time in Adoration since it was all day long. Father Balaji made a quick schedule of what was going to take place before I went up and prayed. It was right after the Benediction when he called me up to the Altar. I couldn't help but to think of the 2 dreams of Father and I in front praying for healing as I walked up to the Altar. We then called the parishioners who were there up to the front. There were about 15 people there. Father Balaji took the lead in praying and then I transitioned in invoking the Holy Spirit calling for healing for all those whom were present.

I prayed for about 10 minutes or so. After the Adoration ended, some people came up to me thanking me for the prayers. I was happy that I was doing what the Lord was calling me to do.

The following months, the prayers were a little more

intense and more towards specific healing of certain illnesses. People would still come up afterwards and thank me for the prayers. One parishioner came up to me and asked me if what I had prayed was scripted. I said no that it was just inspired by the Holy Spirit. He said that he had never heard such a beautiful and inspiring prayer. His look of wonderment was humbling. I told him it was all the Holy Spirit and nothing of my doing.

I pray that eventually the "laying of hands" and full on healing Masses will come. Father Balaji suggested that perhaps restarting a prayer group would be beneficial in praying for people in this way. I told him that I didn't know, that perhaps it was possible down the line. My schedule was pretty full in terms of work and my Church obligations.

I pray that whatever the Lord wills for me to do in this healing ministry, that it will be fruitful. In regards to my disease, it's still with me as of the writing. I know I will be healed but it's in God's time and not mine. I believe in His words "heal so I can heal".

We are called to be "healers" as Father Balaji said. We just have to be open to it.

Chapter 7: My Greatest Gift

I ended my previous book with a social media post about "My Greatest Gift", detailing the "gift" from the Holy Spirit in which I consider to be the one above all the rest, the "gift" of "seeing" death come to people before it happens. The reason for this "gift" is to pray for mercy on their behalf to Our Lord. In particularly the Lord's promise of great mercy through the recitation of Chaplet of Divine Mercy if prayed for the dying.

There have been more occurrences of these particular "visions" since the publication of my first book in which I will recount here.

The first family death that I "received" was in 2006. This was very early on in my conversion.

I "received" this thinking it was something else besides death at first, because it "felt" different from what I had been "receiving" from Our Lord.

This strong disturbance felt more personal. I believe that's what threw me off at first. The disturbance became so strong that it scared me. The "feeling" grew in intensity over the course of the week and it finally peaked on a Sunday morning before the Spanish Mass.

I had told my mother the "feeling" had become very intense to the point where it was affecting me a great deal in terms of stress. My mother and a family friend, who was a part of our prayer group, suggested that we go to the Chapel to pray over this "feeling".

We all 3 knelt by the Tabernacle where Our Lord is present, and we began to pray with great intensity. I was "given" to discern that indeed this intense disturbance was death. Who's death though? A few days later we would find out.

My mother got a call from her aunt in Mexico that her brother, my mother's uncle, was gravely ill. He was on his deathbed.

My mother and her younger sister were raised by their grandparents on their mother's side. My mom's aunts and uncles lived there as well during their upbringing.

This was the impeding death I had "received". It felt so personal because it was a family member, someone who had been close to my mother.

My mom's uncle led a rough life. He despised the Catholic Church and he equally despised Her priests. I believe the intensity of the "feeling" was also because this man needed a lot of prayers before his time was up. I prayed very hard for this man. I offered many Chaplets of Divine Mercy on his behalf.

He was refusing to receive his final Sacraments before the inevitable occurred. He didn't want a priest at his side. His ill will towards the Church was his reasoning.

God is Merciful though, he allowed me to "receive" this death in order for His Divine Mercy to flourish.

My mother got another call a few days after the initial

call, informing her of her uncle's passing. They told my mother that the impossible occurred right before his passing though. Her uncle suddenly had a change of heart out of the blue and asked for a priest. He was able to make a Confession and receive his final Sacraments. They said he passed on with a peaceful smile on his face, a far cry to what he was exhibiting a couple of days earlier.

A miracle had occurred and the Lord had allowed me to be a part of that! God is so good!

My mother was somewhat surprised of this supernatural occurrence, which led to this miracle. I don't believe it ever occurred to her that something like this would come from one of children or much less from anyone else close to her.

This case, is one I gave testimony to when we had our first Divine Mercy celebration a few years later. May the Lord and His Mercy be praised forever!

In another case, which happened on a Divine Mercy Sunday, occurred in a couple of years ago.

The last few years, we have moved the Divine Mercy Sunday celebration to the big Church from the Chapel. I usually give testimony and a reflection after we pray the Chaplet of Divine Mercy.

While we were praying the Chaplet in this particular case, I kept "feeling" something approach me from behind on my left side. I kept looking back over my shoulder by instinct because of this "feeling". I "knew" it was a spirit of some kind. It was something that was trying to get my attention. I prayed for whatever it was during the Chaplet, and I didn't think much more of it afterwards because I was in charge of the whole celebration and I had a lot to take care of. A few days later I got a call revealing what this "spirit" was.

A parishioner from our Church called me saying that her longtime boyfriend had just died unexpectedly. She asked if I had "received" his death. She had heard some of my testimony and she was a little familiar with what I am "given" to do by Our Lord. While I was listening to her, all the pieces came together. The spirit I "felt" that Divine Mercy Sunday was death and the "feeling" being behind me and to my left was precisely where this woman was sitting during the Divine Mercy celebration. I told her what I had "felt" after she had finished speaking. I told her that I had indeed prayed for him and his soul. I don't know if she totally comprehended this through her grief stricken state.

Once again the Lord showed His great mercy, specifically on this man's soul, I believe this woman's constant prayers for her boyfriend is the reason the Lord allowed me to "receive" this and pray for mercy for him.

This coming of the "spirit of death" to me has occurred more times than I can remember. This is one of the ways the Lord presents death to me so I can pray for souls. When it's more that one death occurring, these "spirits" come accordingly. I just "know" that it's more than one death coming. I also "know" that it's not occurring at the same time but in close timing of each other. I find it amazing how the Lord allows me to discern this. It's nothing of my doing of course.

An example of this occurred in the Spring of 2015. I was in the new Church hall on a Wednesday night after Youth Group when I "received" multiple "spirits". I was speaking to the then Youth Director when I "felt" 2 spirits come to me. It's always very distinct in their "feel" but not so in the degree of how I "feel" in its presence. At times I immediately know it's death and others it's a fleeting feeling that doesn't linger. In either case, I always pray for mercy immediately because I know what's coming, death. In this case it was one of our former parish priest and a long time member of our Church. They both passed just days after I "received" these "spirits".

In this case, I "received" this at the Church, which usually means it's someone from our parish. Like in the case of the woman's boyfriend I just recounted, the "feeling" occurred in Church and it's because the person who passed was very close to this parishioner.

These "spirits" that come to me that signal death specifically of a parishioner or those very close to them, only occur when I'm at Church or dream about the Church or the parishioners. Other times when I'm outside the Church and these "spirits" come, it's never a death of one of my fellow parishioners.

There's usually some connection to whoever is going to die when I "receive" death. I'm connected in many ways to it.

In the case of the Tennessee bus crash in late 2016 that claimed the lives of 6 children, I "received" a connection via a dream.

I had a dream just a day or so before the fatal crash. In the dream, I see multiple small coffins on each side of me stacked on top of each other as I entered this dark damp room. As I awoke from the dream, I "knew" that the death of children was coming and coming soon. The small sized coffins in the dream was the connection to this tragic event.

I use to stress out in thinking that I couldn't miss any detail in my dreams or in something that came upon me in my waking life that I needed to pray for. Any death that came that didn't ring a bell; I would scour my journals to see if perhaps I overlooked it. After some time, I know the Lord in His infinite Mercy allowed me the discernment necessary to pray for these souls. Nothing was overlooked. I had to trust the Lord in that. I was looking too much in myself in these matters and not nearly enough in the Lord. Jesus, I trust in You!

As I described in the first book, the Lord presents death to me in many ways. I really don't know the reason why. Perhaps it's to keep all the "gifts" active by having to use the different ones to "receive" death.

One of the ways I "receive" death, which has been occurring a lot more now at this point of my journey, is when a lot of people are affected by it. Meaning that a particular person is known by a large group of people. It's not necessarily a celebrity when this happens, even though that's occurred multiple times.

There was a young man who passed away in early 2018 in my hometown, that I "received" just moments before the death occurred. Seeing the large outpouring about the kindness of this young man on many social media posts following his death, connects this particular way of "receiving" death.

The moment I recognized it was death was just before midnight. The "feeling" though, began just before 5pm. It was triggered by someone who was surprisingly angry with me for some reason. That "feeling" then turned into a long afternoon and evening of thinking about what had occurred with this person. It bothered me. That afternoon at work and then later that evening at youth group at the Church, this "feeling" was building within me. As midnight approached, I was drained and the "feeling" of death was strong. I had to focus to pray at that point. I didn't want to pray but I forced myself to pray. I prayed the "Chaplet" for this impeding death. I was exhausted spiritually, mentally, and physically.

The next day, in the afternoon, the news of this young man's death was all over my social media feed. It took a few minutes of searching to discover the timing of this young man's death; it was 10 minutes past midnight. He passed away in a car wreck. I "knew" the soul whom I prayed for in my exhausted state the night before was his. A little digging on this young man's social media page, I came to recognize who he was.

In 2013, this young man came along with some other local high school students, to help in a charity run that took place on my family's land. This young man had drastically changed his look since that that day. I do remember seeing him on a couple of occasions after that. He was easy to spot because of his very lean and very tall stature. I know the Lord had mercy on him because He allowed prayers of mercy to be prayed before his death. Thank you Lord! I didn't tell anyone about what I "received" about his death except for a friend of mine.

I was messaging a friend telling them about what I had "received" about this when I was given to "know" that another one of theses types of death was about to occur. A death where many people were impacted. Once again I was exhausted, more so than the previous death. I was still able to offer up prayers for this impending death before I went to sleep. Sometime in the afternoon the next day, I read about this young seminarian that was studying in Rome who had passed away. This young man was very well known in the Catholic social media circles because he was very active online. He had a book out as well. I did see him on some online videos he posted very shortly before his passing. Most of the Catholic social pages I follow commented on his passing. The young seminarian was friends with so many of them. I "knew" this is what I was given to pray for. I know my prayers weren't needed in his case because of the very holy life he was leading. I know the Lord showed this faithful servant of His tremendous mercy. May the Lord in His infinite mercy be praised!

Very shortly after this, another death was "shown" to me. This one was a suicide that made news in the local paper. Not much information was given on this particular soul but I knew the timing and the prayers I offered were for this death. The intense despair that invaded my soul out of nowhere was my indicator that a soul was soon about to pass via suicide. I prayed for mercy for this soul and this intense feeling very quickly left after I had prayed. The despair had lasted for hours though before it left in an instant after my prayers were completed. That was another sign that this was a supernatural event from Above.

All 3 of these deaths happening in succession were very taxing on me but I thank God for allowing me to pray for mercy on these 3 souls.

Something that's been somewhat new since my pilgrimage to Medjugorje that I took in March 2018 in regards to "receiving" impending deaths, has been the way I feel physically when I "receive" them.

The several deaths since Medjugorje have completely drained me physically. I've experienced being drained after I've prayed over multiple people in the past but this new feeling is on another level. In Scripture, (Luke 8:43-48) a woman touches Our Lord while He was walking among a large crowd and He asks, "Who touched me? Someone has touched me; for I know that some power has gone out from me." The woman who touched Our Lord believed that just by touching Him she would be healed. Jesus said that her faith had healed her. I knew that there was Scriptural reference to what I was feeling early on in my journey after I had prayed over many people.

One instance came in April of 2018. I was heading to the new Prayer Garden and Grotto at our Church on a Sunday afternoon to go get ready for our weekly Sunday Rosary. I realized when I got the Church parking lot that I had forgotten the speaker that I use to play music for the Rosary. I was just about to get out of my car when I was "given" to know what it was that I had been "feeling" all day and the reason I had forgotten the speaker. The Lord was presenting to me an impending death to pray for. I hadn't prayed the Chaplet of Divine Mercy at that point since I was feeling completely drained of energy and I "felt" heavy all day. I was going to wait until later before bedtime to pray it but I "knew" that the drive back home to pick up the speaker was the time I needed to use to pray the Chaplet for a soul. I was amazed how the Holy Spirit prompted me to pray by allowing me to forget the speaker at home, which I hadn't done before. I prayed the Chaplet on my drive back and prayed for this soul. I was still drained the rest of the day and the first part of the next day, which was Monday when we received the news of a death that occurred close to the family. I "knew" that death was what I "received" the day before. I thank God for allowing me to pray as I did for this soul. Perhaps I wouldn't have prayed as well for this soul if it weren't for the prompting of the Holy Spirit the day before. It wasn't until the next death that I "received" that I realized that there was a correlation between this extreme draining I was feeling and a death that was about to occur.

It was a very short time later that once again I felt completely drained despite being well rested. I couldn't figure out why I felt like I did. Some "feeling" of sadness was with me as well but I was more focused on the draining. I was still able to pray well that day despite how I felt. I went to sleep that night like normal but I was awakened in the middle of the night by this soul wrenching pain. I got up and realized what this pain was. It was death. I was so exhausted that I could only pray about a minute's worth of pray for this soul. I prayed, "sorry Lord that's all I can offer for this soul". I fell back asleep. In the early afternoon, I received a message about a death of a baby that had just occurred earlier that morning. We knew the family of whom this baby belonged to pretty well. I was saddened by this death to say the least. This death was pretty extreme in terms of being drained on top of the sadness that was attached to it. When I learned of this death and realizing that I was given to "receive" it the day before, all the feelings that were still lingering left. My energy came back to normal. My "power" so to speak was restored.

The other death that came where I felt drained came just after the death of the baby. This occurred in May of 2018. Once again the "feelings" like before were present but with a sense of something unclean. It made me feel as though I needed to go to confession. I had already planned to go but this "feeling" put a lot of doubt in my head. This ugliness within me made feel miserable as well. Once again by the prompting of the Holy Spirit, I prayed for whoever it was that was needing Divine Mercy from Our Lord Jesus. I prayed the Chaplet of Divine Mercy while I walked to Church as I was out of town for one of my niece's college graduation. I walked about a mile as I prayed under the warm Sun of Central Texas. I made it to the Church and waited about 10 minutes before it was my turn to enter the Confessional. I made a good Confession by the grace of God and I continued to pray in this Church dedicated to Our Lady. I prayed quite a bit and I just sat in the presence of the Lord as Mass was still over an hour away from starting. I felt better after Mass was over and my energy returned like the previous times. The next day the news of a coordinated suicide bombing in some Catholic Churches in Indonesia that killed around 10 souls and injured dozens more made world news. The Holy Spirit confirmed to me that what I "received" the day before with the "feelings" I had was this horrible attack. I believe that's why I "felt" this unclean "feeling" because of the evilness that was about to take place just a couple of hours later.

I'm not sure why this new way of "receiving" death was given to me. Perhaps it's a progression of sorts. It could be like Our Lord and this "power" within me has to be used to help these souls. It's nothing of my doing of course. It's all by God's grace. Whatever the reason, I know it's what the Lord is asking of me and so I accept it.

In 2015 or 2016, I had a dream of a banker from my hometown that my family had done business with for a very long time. This banker had long retired at an early age though. I would see him on occasion at the local superstore. In the dream though he was still working at the bank. It struck me very odd to see him in my dream. When I awoke, I wondered why he was in the dream but as I usually do, I prayed for him and his family. I prayed a Chaplet of Divine Mercy for him. When I would see him around after this dream, I would remember the dream and wonder why I was "given" to see him.

After some time, I was attending daily Mass as I do, and his name was mentioned during the prayers for the sick. I inquired after mass why he was mentioned and I was told that he had terminal cancer.

I did some digging on social media and found one of his daughter's social media page. On her page, I found out that he wasn't doing well and was in tremendous pain. Scrolling back on her page, I read that the cancer was diagnosed about a year earlier I believe. This diagnosis was exactly around the time of the dream. I "knew" at that moment why I had dreamt him. This man and his family were Catholic but didn't attended Mass and it was very rare if we did see them there. I kept praying the Chaplet of Divine Mercy for him all the way to his passing after I learned of his terminal cancer. I believe he needed a lot of prayers before his death and that was why I was "given" to see him in this dream. I believe someone or maybe multiple people, had been praying for the salvation of this fallen away Catholic. The Merciful Lord in His Infinite Mercy allowed prayers of mercy to said on his behalf before his passing. I believe his tremendous suffering at the end was redemptive suffering. I know without a doubt that God granted mercy on this man at the time of his death. May God be praised!

A recent case that occurred in July of 2018 was one that was unique in terms of the way I "received" it. At first it was very similar to the many cases I've written about in these testimonies of mine. The disturbance in my soul was on par with the others but it did linger for about 5 days though. I became irritable as the "feeling" was at its strongest on a Tuesday morning. At lunchtime, I described this "feeling" to a family member as a sharp pain and hurt piercing my soul. I further explained that I had to offer this "feeling" for a soul. I prayed the Chaplet of Divine Mercy as I usually do in these cases but this "pain" lingered the rest of the week. I kept praying the Chaplet for whose ever soul was needing it.

By that Saturday evening the "pain" and the rest of effects of "receiving" death, was once again peaking. I was so exhausted by the end of the day that I was struggling praying for this soul. I "knew" I had to pray the Chaplet of Divine Mercy once again for this soul but I was too tired spiritually, mentally and physically to pray it. As I was getting ready to go to sleep, I believe the Holy Spirit allowed me to start the Chaplet for this soul. It was nothing of my doing. I was surprised that the Our Father, which is the opening prayer of the Chaplet, came out of my mouth.

The strange and unique thing about this case was that after the beginning part of the Chaplet, this anxiety was building within me. It felt like trying to finish this prayer of mercy, was a long task to complete. My breathing began to quicken as I was getting closer to the finishing. By the time I reached the closing of the prayer, it felt like I was about to get into a full fledged panic attack. By the grace of God though, I fell asleep just minutes after finishing. This pending panic attack was stopped by the Lord in its tracks.

The next morning, which was Sunday, began normally. I felt no ill effects of that previous night as I went to morning Mass and then to lunch with my family. After lunch as I got home, I received the news of a death of a long time member of our Church. This man whom I knew since I was child was just a little older than I was. He graduated High School just a year before I did. He had moved away about an hour or so from our hometown but his siblings still live here and attend Mass along with his nieces and nephews. I've gotten to know his family here quite well in recent years through my activities in the Church.

I "knew" the moment I heard the news of his death that it was his soul whom I first "received" earlier in the week. He passed away from a heart attack early Sunday morning and was found in his bed. I believe what I felt with that incredible anxiety and my struggling to pray for a soul the night before, was because his death was just hours away. I "received" his death on a Tuesday and by God's infinite mercy, I was able to offer many prayers on his behalf prior to his passing early Sunday morning,

I've been praying for some of the younger members of his family on a regular basis for many years now. I believe that's why I was "connected" with this death. Perhaps it was why it was a little more intense than some other cases. Nevertheless, I know the Lord had mercy on his soul upon his passing. I thank the Lord for His infinite Mercy.

I went to his viewing at the funeral home a week later and all I could think about was what the Lord had allowed me to "receive" prior to this man's passing. I was taken aback at the reality of it all. May His Mercy be praised forever!

In mid-2017, I was looking back on some messages I had sent to a friend, and I discovered that I had a relayed an account of a "death dream" to her that ended up being prophetic but I didn't know it at the time. That death was that of my brother.

In the dream, I see that my brother is dying but he's walking around and looking well. The "feeling" was like there was a time limit on him and when the time was up, that was when he was going to die. I would think about that fact in the dream and I would cry. Then I learn in the dream that my dad has 6 months left to live. I'm then at a grocery store and I see Juana, a former Confirmation student and former aide of mine, with her mother checking out. I notice everything that Juana was wearing because it stuck out for some reason. I tell her that I needed to talk to her but she didn't want to talk to me until I told her that my brother was dying and my father had only 6 months to live. We then proceeded to leave in a car together and at that point I woke up.

The next morning I see on one of my social media sites in the news feed section, that Juana's sister posted a picture of Juana and herself and in the picture and Juana is wearing the exact same outfit from the dream.

When I re-read this dream I sent to this friend of mine, I realized that my brother died just short of the 6 months that I had mentioned in the dream. My brother like the dream was walking around ok before he got sick very quickly and passed away. He did have a real time limit on him and the Lord "showed" me via this dream. I know I prayed for him right after the dream but I had forgotten about the dream until I came upon it again over a year later.

Juana, my former student from this dream, is a person in whom the Lord has used to show me some very significant events on my journey including the 2017 massacre in Las Vegas.

Chapter 8: Juana

On October 1, 2017, 58 people were killed in Las Vegas, Nevada in one of the largest mass shootings in US history. A shooter from a nearby hotel room, shot down on a crowd at an outdoor concert. I believe that a couple of days earlier there was a sign in my dream that marked this impending tragedy. This young woman named Juana, who was in my 2nd year Confirmation class, was in this dream and in 2 other situations aside from my brother's death dream. Juana also played a part that marked some major events.

Juana was also my assistant in my 7th year Confirmation class. Ever since she was in my class 5 years earlier, she had been in prayers. She is one of the souls in whom the Lord granted me a "connection" in which I described in my first book.

The first occurrence that involved Juana took place prior to the Las Vegas shooting happened on December 2015 in an East London Underground Station. In that attack, 3 people were seriously injured by a man wielding a knife. I saw the pictures of the attack on a news website and the images instantly looked familiar.

Very shortly before the attack, I had a dream of "The Tube" as they call the London station. In the dream I see 2 policeman dressed in riot gear. One of the policemen was Juana, the "connection".

I prayed as I do when I dream of such places, because

it almost always signals something very significant. There were no deaths but only serious injuries. Thank God!

Were these prayers that were offered up to the Lord prior to this attack in order to prevent these potential deaths from occurring? It's not the first time something like this has happened.

Around 2010 or so, my parents and I went to house of some friends to pray. During my years in the prayer group, my parents and I frequented houses of some friends of ours to pray. We would eat and converse at first and then we would get into some deep prayer.

I always looked forward to these occasions because the visions I "received" during these prayers sessions were always powerful. This particular session was no different.

We were in a prayer circle holding hands in this large house that sits about 15 miles from where we live. It was perhaps my father who took lead during this prayer time when this powerful vision came to me. It was a vision of death. The "feeling" was so clear and distinct. I just didn't know whose death it was initially. I opened my eyes and looked around the prayer circle to see if the Lord would reveal to me if it was someone within the circle. I closed my eyes again and asked the Lord to show me whose death it was I was "feeling". He showed me. It was one of the ladies in the circle of about 10 people. She kept flashing in my mind. It then became clear it was her or someone in her family. The "feeling" was so strong that it visibly affected me. I felt awful because the death felt so real as it does when I "receive" it. A stream of tears began to fall. I told the group after we finished what I "received" but didn't specifically say it was death. I told this woman that it had something to do with her. She told me to relay this vision to her but in private. So my mother and I and this woman, and one other person went to another room and I told her what I had just "received".

I made sure to stress to her that it was most likely a family member of hers and not herself. I believe that "feeling" would've been even stronger or somehow different had it been her. She took the vision with great faith to my surprise and said she was going to pray fervently on it.

It was so strange to me that she received this vision with great faith. I was so use to a lot of rejection and hostility with relaying these types of visions up to that point.

About a week or 2 went by and this woman told us that this vision I "received", came to pass but with a different end.

She said she got a call from some family members in Mexico, from a heavily Cartel occupied area where they live, and told her what had just occurred.

She was told that the Cartel sent some people to their house there in Mexico to go kill a male family member. This family member had been involved in some way with the Cartel. The order had come down to murder him. They busted into the house but didn't find this man. The family from Mexico said it was a miracle that he didn't get killed.

The woman, our friend, said she knew about the situation beforehand because I had told her about the vision I "received" about them. She told them that it was because of our prayers that this family member wasn't killed, that God's incredible Mercy intervened. Praise the Lord!

I believe this was like the London Tube case. God's ways are far beyond our ways.

The 2nd case in which Juana, who was now my assistant in my class at this point, played a major role in God's infinite Mercy saving a soul, was the case from my first book, the suicide which I "received" in the Spring of 2016.

She was the "trigger" that led to the "feeling" of impending death, the eventual suicide I "received" in real-time. That was one of the most profound experiences I've ever had on this journey of the Lord. That death/suicide took a while for me to recover from.

The "trigger" began with seeing a picture of her on social media and then continuing with her failing to answer a plea for prayers when this "feeling" of death was beginning to overwhelm me. Had not the "trigger" with just a simple picture of her occurred, would this agonizing soul have received those heartfelt prayers of mercy just minutes before his death? God only knows such things. I just know that God's infinite Mercy prevailed and that's all that matters.

The 58 souls of Las Vegas also had prayers of mercy said on their behalf before this tragedy took place.

When I saw the aftermath of this tragedy online and on all the news channels as the rest of world did, the images I saw were straight from the dream I had a couple of days earlier.

Juana who at the time of the tragedy, was no longer my assistant, was the main person in this dream. The "connection" to the tragedy was of a commercial plane in the dream that seemed to be out of place. The plane was in such close proximity to this city we were in. I was walking behind Juana when I noticed the huge out of place commercial airplane. The plane appeared to be cut in half. It got my attention like it was something I needed to see and I just glared at it. In the morning as I awoke, I "knew" it had meaning. I "knew" it was a tragedy that was approaching fairly quickly. My initial thought was that it was an impending plane crash. The plane wasn't wrecked in the dream though, just cut in half. I was trying to analyze the dream. I then just realized that I needed to pray for whatever was coming. I prayed for mercy for how many ever souls were going to perish.

Looking at the images of this tragedy online, I saw the plane I saw in my dreams. The outdoor concert arena, the hotel where the shooter committed the heinous act, was right next to the airport. I could see from the pictures how the airport and the big commercial planes were visible from that area. It was eerie seeing how similar it was to the dream.

The Holy Spirit confirmed to me that what I "received" in the dream, was indeed this tragedy. Many years of living this "supernatural" life, I know that God uses many ways to save souls.

To some people perhaps, they may think "that's a stretch" in my recounting and making a connection in "receiving" this Las Vegas tragedy but I know the Lord works in this incredible way in allowing His Mercy to reign. I believe with my previous book and this one, I've presented enough testimony and proof to that account. God's Mercy is never to be underestimated in the saving souls even in the most horrific of situations such as that tragedy in Las Vegas.

The last major occurrence that involved Juana was the profound tragedy on May 18, 2018, the school shooting of Santa Fe, Texas. The shooter killed 10 students and injured 10 more. These school shootings have become way to common but God's Divine Mercy prevailed for these souls in Santa Fe upon their tragic deaths.

On Wednesday, 2 days before the tragedy, I dreamt of Juana once again. Given the previous deaths I "received" when it involves her in some way, I "knew" a tragedy was close. The dream gave hints of what was to come just 2 days later.

In the dream, I see Juana amongst a chaotic scene where I saw some men carrying assault rifles and a lot of people running around terrified. I remember seeing law enforcement there as well. Everything was black in color. The clothes that everyone had on, to the vehicles that were there in this dream were black. The sky itself had a dark tint to it. Juana and I were 2 of the people who scrambling around in this chaos.

As I woke, I knew this dream was a prophetic one. I prayed a Chaplet of Divine Mercy for the souls that were going to be involved in this impending tragedy. I had no doubt it was going to something public but I didn't know what.

The next day, the day before the shooting, all the signs of an approaching death hit me pretty strong.

I felt drained all day and I started to "feel" this sadness building within me. Trying to get through my prayers seemed like a chore but I was able to pray all 20 Mysteries of the Holy Rosary. Frustration was beginning to sit in as well. This "feeling" within me then started to make feel so much negativity within my thoughts. My work and the people around me started irritating me. I was on the verge of telling my sister Maria who was working with me, that a death was coming and it was close. At that point the frustration turned into an extreme sadness. I had to quickly regain my composure and focus on praying at that moment or I would've broken down crying right there. It was too difficult to continue working but I was able to finish my work by the grace of God. I prayed a couple of more Chaplet of Divine Mercy for these souls that I was "feeling", as I knew death was close.

By the time I went to bed, I was so drained that I was only able to offer a few short prayers for these souls.

In the morning, I went to daily Mass and then to work for a bit. I had absolutely no energy. When I walked, I felt extremely heavy. As I got home by late morning, the news broke of the school shooting in Santa Fe, Texas. I immediately "received" the knowledge from the Holy Spirit that what I had "received" through the dream with Juana in it and all I "felt" the day before and early that morning was this tragedy. It was somewhat strange feeling this confirmation from the Holy Spirit within my soul and at the same time feeling upset and angry of what had occurred in this school.

I know the Lord had mercy on these precious young souls when they passed on. I have no doubt about that. In the end evil didn't prevail, the mercy of the Lord did.

It's fascinating to see how many events the Lord used Juana to "show" me what was coming in order for me to pray. She is the only one that the Lord has used more than once to "show" me "things" on my journey. There's a reason I believe He has done this. I hope Juana will be able discern this reason on her own. Until then, I will continue praying for her.

Chapter 9: Confirmation

In 2009, I was asked by a friend to help her in teaching the Confirmation class at my parish. It was an exciting proposition for me, the chance to start teaching all that I had learned in the first few years of my journey.

The previous Confirmation class had my "fingerprints" on it, in terms of the Saint names the class chose.

The candidates choose a Saint in whom they can relate to and turn to in prayer. They are their intercessor in Heaven. Hopefully these young men and women will aspire to imitate these holy souls in the way they live.

The friend who asked me to help her teach, was already helping with the previous year's class. She asked me for a book of Saints or suggestions for Saint names for the candidates.

Ideally this process of choosing Saint names should've been done during the religious school year, with a lot of prayer and research involved. It shouldn't have been done just days before these candidates were to receive this Sacrament.

I sent her a list of Saints that at that point of my journey, I had been researching and reading about. When the program for the Confirmation Mass was handed out, I found a lot of the Saint names that I had provided were listed with the candidates.

Through all my years of teaching, I still encountered candidates who didn't put much prayer or thought in choosing Saint names despite my constant reminders.

My friend, heading into my first year of teaching, was familiar with my supernatural journey up to that point which was only 3 years in. We made some preparation heading into the new class. I was excited but I was quickly disappointed in what I encountered with that first class.

Their knowledge of their Catholic faith was astoundingly very low. Some of them didn't even know their basic prayers. For a long while after that first class, I blamed myself for not being prepared enough for them. I felt handcuffed so to speak. I couldn't speak to them about my personal experiences because I was told from our then priest, that these kids weren't mentally or spiritually capable of accepting these "experiences" that I had been given. The priest said to me, "you can't give a newborn baby a T-bone steak" and with that I was limited.

Years later I realized that I did the best I could with what I was given. It was a learning experience for me. I thank the Lord for the opportunity He gave me in teaching.

Heading into my 2nd year, I ended up going into alone. There was somewhat of falling out between my friend and I. She never replied to my many attempts in contacting her during the Summer months. She only made contact with me just a week or so before the new class was to begin. I told her that the new class didn't need any negative feelings between us heading into it and she took that in meaning that she was the negative aspect. I was referring to our lack of communication but she quickly took it the wrong way. She dropped out.

I made an effort in preparing for the new class, which was made up of around 35 candidates. It was about 20 more than the first class. I made lesson plans for the whole year prior to starting but something was bothering me as I made the plans. "How can I teach what I prepared without them knowing how the Lord is working in my life" is what I was struggling with. I prayed for guidance, and finally the day before the new class was to begin, I "felt" that the Lord was telling me to give my personal testimony to them. Despite what I was told by the young priest a year earlier, I knew this was the right decision.

The first Wednesday night, the day when we use to hold class in those days, came for the Jr. High and High School kids. My Confirmation classroom was packed. One of my nieces was part of my class as well. She had known part of my testimony but I'm sure she didn't know what I was about to say to them on that first night.

The Holy Spirit was with me when I gave my testimony to those young men and women. I could see their expressions on their faces change as I got into the supernatural aspect of my story. It went from "this class is going be boring" to a perplexing look of "what did I just hear?". I know that night set the tone for the rest of that year. I believe a lot of them took in a great deal of what was taught to them. I know spiritual seeds were planted. Even though I got really sick from my type 1 diabetes the 2nd half of that year and it affected my teaching a bit, it was a good year.

That year by God's grace, I started having prayer sessions with all the classes in the big Church. It was with 7th graders through High School sophomores with a few upperclassmen.

These prayer sessions were very intense. I used my Charismatic Renewal experiences from the prayer group I was in at the time, to help guide me with these youths. As I wrote in my previous book I was able to "receive" many things in terms of relaying "messages" and "knowledge" for them during these sessions.

They took everything in. They were most definitely ready to receive the supernatural despite what I was told otherwise. Many of these youths definitely needed this outlet during these sessions. Most of them had never prayed that much for an extended period of time as we did on those special nights.

I even read an article on how the youth needed to be taught the supernatural in an extensive manner, to bring that aspect of our Church to them. Our Church history is full of the supernatural. It was founded by miracles and those miracles still continue to this day.

I believe we all need to pray that the Holy Spirit opens are hearts and souls completely to the supernatural. Our Lord said that we would able to accomplish even greater things than He did on Earth. We just need to have faith and believe.

During my 4th year, things didn't go as well as they had in year 2 and 3. This class towards the end didn't really come together as my previous classes did. I had some candidates who didn't fully accept the Truth of the Church as I presented it to them. I believe they were use to the water down teachings that unfortunately plagues a lot of Catholics these days. Many are afraid to teach the Truth in fear of offending people. Our job as teachers is to teach the fullness of the Church in all its aspects and not just teach what the candidates want to hear.

I personally do not want to stand in front of Our Lord at my judgement and have to answer for not teaching the fullness of His Church in fear of offending people.

That 4th year class was taken out of my hands towards the end. This class was really unruly. I even dreaded coming in on Wednesday nights at that point.

I had made the decision to quit after that year during the Summer, after I found out that I was going to paired up with a complete stranger that next year.

During the Diocesan Youth Conference that Summer that I had attended with our youth group during my first 6 years in this Ministry, I told the then Youth Director that I was done.

She finally talked me into sticking around for a little while longer to see how this new pairing with this stranger would feel to me. I had every intention of quitting anyway. I went through the motions later on that Summer when these certification classes that we were required to take came around. I met this new guy during these classes. I just couldn't bring myself into quitting as the Summer ended and the new class was about to begin. I realized I was being selfish. I realized that it was all about these kids and not about me, and so I forged ahead.

When this 5th year class began, I started it like I usually did, with my testimony. A friendship began with this new guy named Julian Rios. We ended up becoming very good friends and that 5th year class ended up being a great class. I'm thankful that the Lord allowed me to continue teaching and making this new friendship. It was a great blessing on both parts. Thank you Lord!

My new friend ended up leaving shortly after my 6th year started. I ended up having 6 more helpers over the next couple of years. Aside from Juana whom I wrote about in the previous chapter, no one lasted a full year with me. I'm not sure why it has worked out like that. God only knows.

I don't know how long the Lord will allow me to teach but I will do my very best in teaching His Truth until He says that's enough. I know that teaching is one of my missions. I've grown as a teacher by His grace. These young men and women have truly been a blessing in my life.

Chapter 10: "Supernatural Empathy"

As I wrote in my first book, this "Supernatural Empathic Gift" that the Holy Spirit has granted me, has continued to be constant through these first 12 years in this "life"

This "Empathic Gift", is a gift in which the Holy Spirit allows me to take on and absorb other people's feelings and emotions and feel them as though they were of my own. I'm not sure when I was given it, but I do know that one of my first realizations of it was in 1997.

Princess Diana of Wales had just passed away and I was watching her funeral on TV, which was worldwide news at the time. I remember watching the funeral procession, as I'm sure the rest of the world did as well. I was on the floor in my bedroom lying on my side watching it. I'm not sure how long I had been watching the coverage, when all of sudden this wave of hurt and sadness overtook me. I started crying to my surprise. I cried a lot. It was as though I took on all the sadness and the emotions of all the mourners who were there. I was crying as though it was someone I knew personally. It felt that personal to me.

It wasn't until my conversion in 2006 that this "gift" became a constant part of my life. Even with my Confirmation classes throughout the years, this "gift" and the "gift" of "feeling" the condition of souls, has been something that I had to learn how to deal with.

I don't know how many times I came home from my

class or after a prayer session with kids that it didn't linger with me for quite a while after. There were many nights that these "feelings" kept me up all night.

I absorbed a lot of hurt and pain and sadness from so many kids throughout the years. This "empathic gift" was more prominent during the prayer sessions though. The "feeling" of their souls was mainly felt after teaching a class. I would come back home and feel awful afterwards. It wasn't every candidate but "feeling" multiple souls not in a State Of Grace was very taxing on me. It "feels" like I'm so unclean on the inside, like my own soul was exposed to some dirtiness. It's like a stench I cannot smell but can "feel".

There are some days when this absorption of emotions is very vexing. Who am I "feeling"? Who has the Lord sent to me? What exactly is this "feeling"? Why is the "feeling" not going away? All these questions run through my head when these "feelings" seem non-ending. It wears me out at times. Like I've stated before, a lot of times I do not where the line is that separates my feelings and of those I'm "receiving". It's long been blurred. The longer the "feeling" lasts, the more my mind accepts it as my own until the Holy Spirit lifts it from me. The Holy Spirit gives me just enough discernment at that point to offer the person or persons I'm "feeling" up in prayer. Then after I've prayed, the "feeling" is then lifted and peace returns. It's as though I never "felt" anything in the first place.

I do not know if one can truly understand how difficult this "Empathic Gift" can be on someone who's "received" this "gift" from the Spirit of the Lord. Being constantly bombarded with emotions and feelings when one is not feeling well physically or spiritually makes these "feelings" even greater to bear. I trust in Lord though, He knows the perfect time to send me consolation. It may be a small respite at the time but it's the perfect remedy always.

When I have fallen physically ill, everything just "feels" worse. My senses are always heightened in this state. My "defenses" are down so to speak. With this "Empathic Gift", the Lord has called upon not only to "feel" but to also "carry" someone's sickness and not just my own.

One example of this was during my years in the prayer group in my parish. One night as 'I was running on the treadmill at my house, I "received" this great pain in my abdomen. It came in a flash. It was so intense that I had to stop running to gather myself. I was trying to remember if it was something that I had eaten earlier in the day. I just started praying by placing my hand on my abdomen. Within a matter of minutes of praying, this pain left. It was as though nothing had occurred. I was in amazement. I "knew" it was something that was sent by Our Lord at that moment, and not of a natural origin because of how this pain came and left so quickly.

The next day we gathered in the Church hall for our weekly prayer group. We found out from one of the male members that his wife had a miscarriage the day before. He was distraught as you can imagine. At that moment, I "knew" that what I had gone through the night before was his wife's miscarriage. The reason being was to help in "carrying" that pain, not necessarily just the physical pain but the emotional pain that went along with it. I prayed fervently for them. I "received" just a short time later for them, the means in which to pray for healing and the blessing of having another child. I "received" in a vision that they need to seek the intercession of St Jude. The husband received this "message" with great faith. Shortly after this, the wife became pregnant again and had a healthy baby girl a short time later. Praise the Lord!

This "pain" of miscarriage occurred 2 more times after this. They both were very similar in the way I "received" them in the first case. Same reason as before, to help them in "spiritual" sense.

There have been several cases of "receiving" anxiety attacks from other people as well. My own personal anxiety episodes stemmed from medication and the stress of "receiving" so much from Above in terms of intensity.

The first case, I had to go to the ER because this attack came in the middle of the night. I woke up from a deep sleep with my heart feeling like it was about to come out of chest. It scared me because I had never felt anything like that before. Coming out of a deep sleep like that threw my senses off.

The next day, I received a text from someone that they had just gone through an anxiety attack at work and it was pretty intense. They didn't have to be taken to the ER like I was. I believe what I went through was this person attacks. I "received" it before they did. Perhaps it was to lessen their attacks through my "receiving" it first. I absorbed the brunt of it. Even though they said their attack was intense, it would've been a lot worse had the Lord's Mercy not been in play.

These anxiety attacks happened several more times throughout this journey of mine. I prayed with great intensity during these difficult times because I know that's what the Lord was asking of me on these people's behalf. A sacrifice so to speak. Sometimes I wish I could "take on" their entire pain but I know I can't. The Lord doesn't ask that of me.

As I've written before on this empathic subject, I often "receive" people's feelings before they receive it. It's always confirmed to me very shortly after from the person who was ultimately the person who was in need of this sacrifice and prayer. It never ceases to amaze me how the Lord works in me in this way.

The despair I believe, is the worst of the empathic feelings I "receive". To feel the hopelessness of the person is very draining on me, not only spiritually but mentally as well.

There were a ton of cases in which the hopelessness was extreme. The most extreme were the suicides I "received". The case that I wrote about in my first book was the most extreme. To "feel" as though I'm the one who is about to take my own life and "feeling" the exact moment of death of the person who did, is something I don't think I can fully express in words. I know the despair was beyond anything I had ever gone through. The other suicides weren't as extreme but draining nonetheless.

One case in early 2017 was that of a young woman whose father passed away very suddenly. I had known her from my pilgrimage group in 2016 to Italy and Poland. I "felt" all the sadness and despair of losing someone. I was all too familiar with these feelings at that point. This case was one of the few things I did "receive" shortly after my brother's passing.

This young woman posted on social media the day after her father's passing announcing his death. Like always, the Holy Spirit confirmed to me that the "feelings" from the previous days were of hers. I "received" them before she did. The "feelings" that I had left the moment the Holy Spirit confirmed it.

Another case took place shortly after that. In that case, I went through the despair and hopelessness and the very precise understanding that it was all aimed towards Our Lord. The "feelings" were also pretty hard on me coming off the previous case I just wrote about. The confirmation on this came via a phone call from this person reaching out to me and telling me exactly what they were going through. It was exactly what I had just gone through. Like the other case, the "feelings" left the moment it was confirmed. I was able to help this person by giving them spiritual guidance and offering many prayers for them.

I'm thankful that I'm able to "share" in my fellow man's burdens in this way. How better else to pray for someone if I know exactly how they're feeling?

I need to walk through the darkness first in order to understand the darkness that others go through.

Chapter 11: The Supernatural

I remember reading a quote somewhere from Saint Padre Pio the 20th Century mystic Capuchin friar, he said something to the effect that if one is given the supernatural from Our Lord that we ought walk in that as though it was our norm. At this point in my life, I don't think I've ever gotten use to accepting it as my norm. It all still amazes me. God's power in our lives is nothing short of miraculous.

In this chapter I will cite some instances where God's power was shown to me.

During Pentecost of 2008, the prayer group had organized a nightlong vigil in the Chapel. Some talks were given by some of the members on the Holy Spirit and on the subject of Pentecost. We also had some praise and worship music, "alabanzas" as we call it in Spanish.

What I first remember from that night was the weather outside. There was a little chill in the air on this very breezy night. It was eerie similar to the dream I had just the night before. Perhaps it was a foreshadowing for what was in store for me this vigil night.

I "received" a vision very early on during the night's Pentecost program, which took my peace away and caused me some interior pain. The vision was of a pierced heart. It was similar to the image of the Seven Sorrows of The Virgin Mary where her heart is pictured with seven swords piercing it, indicating the seven sorrows of the Our Lady based on Holy Scripture.

I drew a picture of the vision, this pierced heart, and but it in my Bible that I had with me. The vision came to pass as very quickly as the source of this "piercing" came in the form of a person. All I'm going to say is that a person from the group, showed up a short time after this vision, and did something to me that betrayed me. I forgave that person for what they did to me. I know that the Evil One used them to get to me. He almost succeeded, but Our Lord's infinite love triumphed that night!

Our Lord Jesus ever present in the Holy Eucharist was brought out and exposed in this large monstrance. We had a Holy Hour of adoration of Our Lord. Some of the members of the group played "alabanzas" and some members were praying out loud with great fervor during this Holy Hour. I know my father was "praying in tongues" close to the altar. It was very intense.

I was gazing at Our Lord in great anguish at this point, as this betrayal was at its peak when His power was manifested to me. This invisible wave of power from the monstrance came towards me as the prayers and music was going on around me. The first wave was a surprise; the second wave was more intense. Tears came streaming down after that. I couldn't control them as I tried to separate my reasoning and my emotions. "Is this really happening?" I thought. The way these waves felt are hard to put into words. All I can say is that they were more intense with each one that came. There were about 5 or 6 of them in all.

All the pain and hurt that I felt were gone in an instant. Love, peace and joy came in at an intense level. I couldn't believe what I had just "experienced". By the end of the night, I joyfully said goodbye to my betrayer as all I felt was love for them.

I don't know why I "experienced" what I did that night. Maybe it was to show me, even though I already believed, that the Lord was truly present in the small white Host. Perhaps it being the vigil of Pentecost, it was a taste of what the Apostles experienced during the first Pentecost when the Holy Spirit came down upon them. Whatever the reasons, it was and incredible night. Thank you Lord!

As I wrote about in my previous book, the Lord has allowed the supernatural to affect my dreams as well.

One of the most intriguing of those dreams involved a newborn baby. In this dream, I'm at a hospital and a newborn baby is being rolled into surgery on a gurney. I stopped the nurses or whomever it was rolling in this baby, and I "lay hands" on the baby and pray.

I remember the baby's face as I'm praying because the baby was just looking at me and being very quiet. This whole scene was very similar to when I was rolled into surgery when I was very young. The long hallways and the metal looking doors heading into the operating room were the same. Perhaps the Lord used that memory as a backdrop for His miracle that was about to take place.

About a week or so later, a social media page was started for a local newborn baby boy who was born with tumors wrapped around his spinal cord. Somehow I came upon this social media page started by his family.

I immediately recognized the baby boy from my dream and the Holy Spirit confirmed to me that it was him. It gave me chills all throughout my body.

The dream happened more that a week before the baby boy was even born, so it wasn't a case that perhaps I came upon this social media page and I subconsciously had it in my mind.

The baby had this incredibly risky surgery scheduled to try to remove the tumors. The prognosis wasn't very good being that the tumors were wrapped around his spinal cord. I just remembered the dream, the "laying of hands", and I "knew" everything was going to be ok. Why else would the Lord give me this dream? Many people were praying for this baby boy and thank God everything went great.

A couple of years have passed since this surgery and some subsequent surgeries, and this little boy has by far surpassed all the doctor's expectations. He's walking and living a normal life. It's by God's infinite mercy that this miracle took place. Praise be to God!

Sometimes the dreams I "receive" from Above are very amusing to me.

This one particular dream I had several years ago is prime example of this.

In the dream, I'm standing outside close to my Church. I then notice a young woman who was in one of my early Confirmation classes walking down the street carrying a freshly baked chocolate cake. I call out to her asking if I could have a piece of cake in which she replied "no!". That was it, nothing more in that dream.

I woke up the next morning and I went to daily Mass that started at 7am. After Mass, I went to Wal-Mart to go buy some things. As I'm walking by close to the women's clothing area, I see the young woman from my dream. I immediately got excited because I had just dreamt her. I stopped her and excitedly told her that I had just dreamt about her. I told her about the chocolate cake and how she refused to give me a piece. She had this very surprised and perplexed look on her face after I told her about the dream. She then tells me with this astonished look on her face, that she was there at Wal-Mart to buy ingredients to make a chocolate cake.

I just smiled and said "wow!". I jokingly then said that she should give me a piece when she was done.

The dream was just a signaling that I needed to continue to pray for her. She has been one of people in whom I pray for on a daily basis now. I can't imagine what she though after that.

There are many dreams like this. The smallest of details in them that come to pass, is enough for me to be in awe of the Lord.

Around 5 years ago, the Lord confirmed to me a vision that I "received" early on in my journey.

During the Confirmation retreats we have just prior to

when the candidates receive their Sacrament, they have been watching a short animated movie called "The Greatest Miracle". The movie depicts what happens supernaturally during the Holy Sacrifice of the Mass. The supernatural accounts shown are from visions given to some of the mystics of the Church. A lot of what is shown is very similar to what I have been given to "experience" as well. This one particular scene depicted in the movie though confirmed a vision I had some years earlier at a Charismatic Renewal Conference I attended with my parents.

In the movie Guardian Angels appear during Mass and take the people, who were praying faithfully, prayer petitions and carrying them up to Heaven. The petitions appeared like glowing spheres. Not everyone's petitions were taken up though because theirs were of a selfish and not thankful manner.

When I first viewed this scene, it was like straight out of that conference years earlier.

During the invocation of the Holy Spirit in this large Catholic High School gym, as I was sitting in the stands praying, I "received" this incredible vision. I was "given" to "see" angels taking petitions from some of those who were praying there and lifting them up to Heaven. I couldn't tell the shape of the petitions that the Angels were taking up but I know they were red in color. Like the movie, not everyone's petition was taken up. What I recall, I would say that about 25 percent of the people's prayers were taken up. This was an incredible sight! I didn't pray for anything because I was entranced by this vision.

I was very happy that this movie confirmed this vision. Joy filled my heart knowing that the Lord allowed me to witness this firsthand. It also brought home the point that we must be thankful and not selfish in petitioning Him. I wonder how many times my petitions weren't carried up because of my selfish nature. Lord have my mercy on me!

There's not a shortage of the supernatural in my life at this point in my life. I use to believe that perhaps if the supernatural hadn't been re-introduced to me, that perhaps I would've never come back faithfully to the Sacraments. There's no point in really pondering that anymore. The Lord reached me and that's all that matters. How it happened is a moot point now.

Chapter 12: Medjugorje

On June 24, 1981, the apparitions of the Blessed Virgin Mary began in a small village in the former Yugoslavia, now named Bosnia and Herzegovina.

Our Lady appeared to 6 children in this unknown village on a rocky steep hill and has delivered numerous messages to the visionaries over these many years.

Medjugorje has received more than it's fair share of criticism over the years. Everything from it being a hoax, to it being a diabolical manifestation.

My first knowledge of the tiny place in South Central Europe was in the 1980's. There were several TV specials during the early years of the apparitions which I remember watching. I know my parents and my sisters were interested in them. My parents even had some Holy Water given to them from Medjugorje in the 1980's. I remember taken some unbeknownst to them and blessing myself with it.

I didn't think too much about Medjugorje after that until my conversion began in 2006.

The advent of the Internet in the 1990's gave the world access to this remote holy place. The apparition events, the moment the visionaries "saw" the Holy Virgin, were recorded and were ready to be played to anyone who wished to view them via the World Wide Web.

I became very curious about these apparition events after my own supernatural path began to unfold in 2006.

Most of the videos I would watch were that of Mirjana Soldo, one of the 6 visionaries. Mirjana receives monthly apparitions on the 2nd of every month and on every March 18th which also happens to be Mirjana's birthday.

Her daily apparitions stopped after 18 months, which began in 1981.

Our Lady wished for these monthly messages to be for those who do not yet know the love of God.

I watched many videos of the apparitions over the years to see if I could "feel" anything at the moment Our Lady "appeared" to Mirjana. I figured I would be able to sense something to confirm to me that she was really appearing in Medjugorje.

I honestly never really sensed anything during these recorded events. That didn't mean that she wasn't appearing there, it just meant that I wasn't "given" the grace to "sense" it in this way. Yet one of her monthly apparitions did confirm a message I "received" from Our Lady back in 2008.

My first intention or aspiration to make a pilgrimage to Medjugorje was in 2012. There was pilgrimage scheduled for the Spring of 2012 by the pilgrimage company we used for our first pilgrimage in 2008 to France. One of the stops in this particular pilgrimage in 2012 was to Medjugorje. I believe it was going to be just a 2-day stop there. Nevertheless I wanted to go.

My oldest sister Maria was diagnosed with breast cancer in January of 2012 and her subsequent surgery in February prevented us from going. I made a personal offering to Our Lady in hopes of making that trip. My prayers were answered, but it took 6 years for it to come to pass.

In those 6 years, my belief that Our Lady was appearing there was met with doubt. Many stories, reports and commentaries against these apparitions appeared online over the years as well. My reading them, allowed doubt to come in.

I really wanted to believe it was true but some of these so-called reports made a good case that it was false. Reporting false facts and claims can strengthen any case if the person trying to determine the validity of a something is debating a certain claim, and in my case the Medjugorje apparitions.

In March of 2017, my parents and I and one of nieces and one my nephews made a pilgrimage Fatima, Portugal for the 100th anniversary of Our Lady appearing to 3 children in 1917. Fatima is an official Catholic Church approved Marian apparition site and as of this writing, Medjugorje is not. It's still under Church investigation but all signs are pointing that it will be an official Marian apparition site.

In the midst of this pilgrimage I asked the priest who was traveling with us about a recent 5-part social media report against Medjugorje that I was reading. His response caught me off guard. I was expecting him to agree with this report for some reason. He said, "if someone says that they see the Holy Mother, who are we to say it's not true". This made a lot of sense to me.

Through my own experiences, people have questioned what I have "received" even though I know with all my heart what I "saw" and "heard" was from God or from Our Lady.

In November of 2016, a month after my brother's passing, my parents and I and 2 of my nephews, made a 2-hour drive North from our hometown to a see documentary on Medjugorje called "Apparition Hill".

"Apparition Hill" which was filmed in 2015 brought together 7 people of different backgrounds and beliefs. There was a widower, a woman with terminal cancer, a drug addict, a man with ALS and a couple of atheists, and a woman who struggled with accepting the Church's teaching of Our Lady.

This film was extraordinary. I won't go into any detail about it here. I hope you all will see it for yourselves. It truly is an incredible and inspiring film.

The desire to visit Medjugorje increased after that, and even more so after purchasing the DVD later and viewing it several more times. I made contact with one of the filmmakers, Cimela Kidonakis, via social media. Cimela actually submitted a video entry when the Film Company was asking for video submissions on why they should be chosen to go to Medjugorje. The chosen "winners", had a 2-week pilgrimage to Medjugorje paid for in order to make this documentary.

She was asked to join the filmmaking process by the director Sean Bloomfield, after her submission wasn't chosen. Cimela has her own production company that is based out of Houston, Texas and Sean was impressed by her work.

I was in contact with Cimela for about a year when the opportunity for me to make this pilgrimage came to pass.

She is so passionate about Medjugorje, which played a key role as well in my making the long awaited pilgrimage to this small village in South Central Europe.

The filmmakers of "Apparition Hill" also offered pilgrimages to Medjugorje. Cimela and her partner Sean Bloomfield led these pilgrimages.

One the incredible blessings of these pilgrimages that they offer, was staying at the hotel/pansion of one of the 6 original seers, Mirjana Soldo.

I very quickly, by the strong calling of Our Lady, was able to book the trip for mid-March of 2018. The trip included being able to be present at Mirjana's annual apparition of March 18. Like I mentioned before, the 18th of March also happened to be Mirjana's birthday. This particular pilgrimage was called "My Heart Will Triumph". It is from Mirjana's title of her first book, an autobiographical account of her life including the incredible insight of a life of a visionary.

After reading Mirjana's book, I was 100% sure that she was totally genuine. Her words erased any lingering doubt that may have been floating around at this point.

I spiritually prepared a few weeks before the trip to be ready for whatever Our Lord and Our Lady had prepared for the group and myself.

The opportunity to meet Mirjana was definitely one of the things I was most looking forward to. Reading her words made feel a connection with her. I felt as though she was an old friend by the time I reached the end of the book.

It felt as though it was a dream as the days leading up to trip quickly passed. I couldn't believe I was actually traveling to Medjugorje!

After a long travel day, our little group of 14 pilgrims arrived in this small village in Bosnia and Herzegovina.

We had pilgrims from California, Florida, Wisconsin and New York and other states. I was the only Texan there aside from Cimela, who hadn't arrived yet.

After an early dinner in our pansion, which is run by Mirjana and her husband Marko, our group leader, Erin Pynes, invited some of us to go climb Apparition Hill where The Queen of Peace first appeared in June of 1981.

It was already dark by the time we made the climb up the rocky hill to the spot where Our Lady first appeared. It had rained by the time we go to Medjugorje and that made the climb a little rough. We used lights from our cell phones to light our way the steep hill. It was an incredible sight to see what I had only seen in pictures and videos, the spot where the Mother of God appeared to 6 children 37 years ago! We all prayed for a bit before we headed down for night.

The next morning at breakfast was the first time I spotted Mirjana Soldo. She was helping serve breakfast to the pilgrims. She only came out briefly a couple of times and she didn't speak to any of us. There were only around 25-30 people there. There was a 2nd group there who joined us through some part of our stay and activities there in Medjugorje.

The daily schedule in Medjugorje usually consists of daily Mass in English in the chapel just outside St James Church. They have other daily masses in different language before and after the English Mass. The evening prayer program begins at 5pm everyday. One of the visionaries said it was Our Lady who requested this. Right before the evening program begins, they have adoration in the chapel from 2-5pm.

The evening program begins with the Sacrament of Reconciliation right at 5pm. There is a long row of outdoor confessional boxes right outside the church to accommodate the many pilgrims from around the world. The many priests, who come here from all over the world as well, are the ones who hear the confessions. The pilgrims just line up in whatever language is available at the time. During the same 5 o'clock hour, the Holy Rosary is being recited inside St. James Church which is the main Church in Medjugorje. 10 decades of the Rosary are prayed before the 6 o'clock International Mass begins. At 5:40pm, everything stops as Our Lady comes. She still appears to 3 of the visionaries daily but in private most of the time now. The church bells ring at that hour and silent prayer is said. The Rosary then continues. After the

International Mass, another 5 decades of the Rosary is prayed along with some other prayers.

A Holy Hour of Adoration is also held several times a week in the Church. It's takes place right after the International Mass at times or a little later from 9pm-10pm.

Daily spiritual talks are also given to the pilgrims throughout the day in a large hall behind St James. Our group attended 2 talks during our stay, which were inspiring and informative.

One of the talks was from a Dominican priest named Father Leon, who also appeared in the documentary "Apparition Hill". He spoke about his own experience of an apparition of Our Lady when he 20 years old. He experienced it when he was a soldier and came on pilgrimage to Medjugorje. I will leave his testimony for the future pilgrim to hear.

Our local guide was Miki Musa. He also appeared in "Apparition Hill". He is the one who writes down Our Lady's message to Mirjana as soon as the apparition ends. Mirjana then gives the message to Miki who quickly gives a rough translation to the pilgrims gathered. The full message in its final translation is given later in the day in multiple languages.

Miki is an incredible guide. He was 9 years old when the apparitions began. He is a very good friend of Mirjana and is very knowledgeable on the history of Medjugorje. He gave us a talk as well. He is very enthusiastic about his faith and is very genuine as well.

He led us up Apparition Hill on our 2nd day of pilgrimage. There are 15 huge stone markers up and down the hill marking the 15 Mysteries of the Rosary. The final 5, the Luminous Mysteries, are behind St James Church. We prayed the Rosary as we made our climb. We stopped at the stone markers and Miki reflected on that particular mystery. It was a very spiritual experience. We then all had plenty of time to pray on our own as we reached the top of the apparition site.

I went to Confession later when the evening program began. I went to an American priest who had received the gift of "Reading of Souls". Pilgrims will encounter many priests with incredible Charisms of the Holy Spirit in Medjugorje. I was anxiously waited for about an hour before it was my turn. In reading about St. Padre Pio who is well known for this particular gift, I was anticipating being "told" something from this American priest.

I'm incredibly grateful that I was able to take part in the Sacrament of Reconciliation in Medjugorje, which is often referred as the "Confessional of the World" but I was disappointed in a way as well. My hopes to have "received" something from this priest with this particular gift didn't pan out. It just wasn't the will of the Lord.

I then went to Mass in the incredibly packed St James Church. I was standing right at the main exit by the one of the doors. It was cold and so I was able to keep a little warm by standing just inside the one closed door. After Mass, Adoration began. I was able to find some of my group and we made our way to the area right in front of the pews. We had an incredible seat in adoring Our Lord ever present in the Holy Eucharist. It was an incredible hour of prayer and adoration. I prayed for everyone who asked me to pray for them before I embarked on my trip. The atmosphere was incredible but the "effect" did not hit me until the middle of night. The openness of my soul during the Holy Hour allowed many things to come in.

As I explained in my first book and in this one about this "Supernatural Empathic Gift" I was given, I became a magnet to the pain, hurt and suffering and other emotions of all the pilgrims that were there adoring Our Lord. Some of the group and myself went out to dinner afterwards and so whatever I "received", didn't manifest itself until my soul was quiet and that was the middle of night while I was in bed.

This deep pain within my soul awakened me, which brought me to tears. I was given to "know" what it was I was "feeling". It was the deep pains that the pilgrims brought with them that night. These pains were of family, health and spiritual problems. I could "feel" and "hear" them crying out to Our Lord. I could "see" them as though I was still present there at St James. I could "hear" the words "why am I here!" over and over. It even came out of my mouth as though it was my own thought. It was a rough night after that. I didn't sleep much and by the time breakfast came around, the "pain" was still lingering. I felt awful. I explained to Erin, our leader, what I had "experienced". She and her friend Leigh, who was on her 2nd pilgrimage to Medjugorje, were incredibly sympathetic and understanding to what I "experienced" on this pilgrimage. I'm very thankful to them. The rest of the group was also very kind and loving. I couldn't have asked for a better group of people to share this incredible journey with.

After I finished breakfast, I went to the lobby and sat in the darkened room while the rest of group was still eating. I was still enveloped in the darkness when I spotted a familiar face across the room sitting on the couch. It was Cimela Kidonakis. She and her filmmaking partner Sean Bloomfield had arrived the night before.

Cimela got up and spotted me and came over and gave me a hug. The "light" this woman carries within her soul, helped the darkness leave. My soul picked up on that quickly. That was definitely a grace from Our Lord. We chatted a bit before we all headed to Mass. By the time morning Mass had ended, the "feeling" of darkness was completely gone. It was as though it was never there in the first place. I felt exhausted though. Having received Our Lord ever present in the Holy Eucharist, I was ready for the day.

We had an opportunity as part of our pilgrimage, to have a question and answer session with Mirjana in her pansion. There were only around 30 of us there and so we had more than the typical amount of time with her. They say that usually the dining area where this takes place is packed with pilgrims and that the Q and A sessions aren't as long as we had that day. The weather was even way better than it was forecasted for our stay. We were incredibly blessed with things like this throughout our trip! Thank you Lord!

I had prepared some questions that I had saved on my phone to ask Mirjana after I read her book but it didn't seem like good questions by the time we got started. A question did come to me though. I asked her what she thought about people, especially online social media reports like I wrote about earlier in this chapter, being so anti-Medjugorje. I said that these came from some so-called orthodox Catholics. Mirjana responded in Croatian and Miki Musa interpreted her response. Mirjana speaks English, but it's easier for her in this format. She said, "they're not Catholic then". She explained that we as Catholics shouldn't criticize or say such negative things about fellow Catholics. If someone says to her that they also "see" the Holy Virgin, she said she first would check it out herself but would be supportive and not criticize. That's what we as Catholics should do, be supportive and not tear down. I then said to her about the doubts I had especially when I would read these "reports" against her and Medjugorje. I told her that after I had read her book, and reading her account about the apparitions and the severe persecution she faced early on, it erased every doubt I had. I told her that her words convinced me. She said many books have been written about her and the apparitions and they never even once approached her about it. These people created many false stories.

She was so sweet and kind to us. She's the "real deal" as they say. She posed for pictures with us and signed our books as well. Some of the group afterwards, told me that I asked a very good question. Sean Bloomfield, who helped Mirjana on her book, told me that Mirjana really appreciated what I said about her book. It was a great experience hearing from a visionary. I honestly can say it was like having a Q and A session with St Bernadette of Lourdes or the Fatima seers.

The group also had the opportunity to climb Mt. Krizevac or as its known to many, Cross Mountain. Cross Mountain is known for its massive 25-ft high cross over looking Medjugorje. Construction of the cross began in 1933 to commentate the 1900th anniversary of Our Lord Jesus' passion and death. The Holy Father, Pius XI, proclaimed 1933 has a jubilee year of the Cross. A relic of the "True Cross" of Our Lord is contained within it. Huge Stations of the Cross plaques are set up all the way up Cross Mountain. It's much more of a climb than Apparition Hill.

Miki our guide led our group in praying the "Stations" as we climbed up this very steep and rocky mountain. We were given plenty of time to pray as we reached the top of the mountain. A couple of pilgrims from our group saw the sun "moving" while we were at the top. The "Miracle of the Sun" which became famous in Fatima, Portugal on October 13, 1917 during Our Lady's Apparition there, is often "experienced" by pilgrims in Medjugorje. I myself didn't see it. It's "shown" to those who it's meant to be for. What an incredible blessing for them!

From the other pilgrimage group, an Eastern Catholic priest, Father Christopher Crotty came along with them. The Eastern Catholic rite is in full communion with Rome. Father Crotty is very passionate and is well educated in the faith. He gave incredible lessons in the Catholic Faith after our days were done. Most of the group gathered as Father Crotty went into some intense teachings. Some even took notes and recorded his talks with their phones. We asked him plenty of questions about the Catholic Faith and he answered them with such great depth. It was fascinating to say the least.

Father Crotty is well known for his healing ministry. I believe he spent around 18 years in this ministry. He's now as of this writing living a monastic life. He did although, give many in our group a healing service in the small chapel of the Two Hearts pansion. Our group was moved to the Two Hearts from Mirjana's pansion to make way for a large group of Italian pilgrims coming in. The Italians are probably the biggest group of pilgrims who comes on pilgrimage to Medjugorje since it's just across the Adriatic Sea.

When our healing service began, Father Crotty first explained to us about healing. There are 3 forms of healing he said, the spiritual, physical and moral healing. He then did some Eastern Catholic chants and their forms of prayer, which is prayed in quick succession. We then repeated some of the responses in chant. He then blessed us all with some anointing oil. I don't remember the specific name of it but it had a beautiful aroma. He then had us line up side by side for those of us who didn't have a chair in this small chapel. He proceeded to "lay hands" on us. Many fell because they were "resting in the spirit". It's more commonly known as "slain in the spirit" but Father Crotty doesn't like to refer to it as that. He said it sounded violent for the Holy Spirit to "slain" someone.

I was next to Cimela when Father got to me. I didn't "rest" as most others had; I didn't "fee" anything until he moved on. I knelt and then that's when I "received" a powerful vision.

I heard Our Lord say to me, "don't you trust Me?" a couple of times. He was wearing a white robe with a red sash and I said, "I do Lord". I believe that it was in reference to one of the reasons of my coming to Medjugorje, to be healed of the Type 1 Diabetes. I've been praying so much for it that I eventually strayed in trusting Him in knowing that He's heard my petitions and will answer them. He then "showed" me a very large crowd of people off to my right side. He just stretched out His arm pointing to them. Our Lord didn't say anything but I "understood" what I was being "shown". The Lord was "showing" me all the people who I was going to encounter in the future who I was going to pray over. It was to pray for healing to be exact. This powerful vision came with the pain and suffering of all these souls. It made me cry because it was overwhelming. The tears just started just like that.

The pain of these souls gave way to this great peace. What an incredible vision! I know that there's work to be done in terms of being used as instrument of the Lord's healing. As poor of an instrument as I am, the Lord's Mercy will still triumph.

Father Crotty said the effects of the healing prayers, are gradual. He said we all must continue to pray to the Holy Spirit to complete our healings.

I was able to speak to Father Crotty alone a few days before this service about healing, in regards to what I "received" as wrote about earlier in this book. His response was to let the Holy Spirit work. Allowing the Spirit to work will open me up to more Charisms needed for my own ministry. His message, and the one message that was prevalent during this pilgrimage was, have an open heart. Complete openness to Our Lord, and to the Queen of Peace will allow miracles to take place. One of the biggest healings taken place in

Medjugorje is the one of the heart. There are plenty of miraculous physical healings that take place here but it's the one of the interior that matters most.

March 18, the day of Mirjana's yearly apparition finally arrived. From her previous messages, we will know in time why March 18th was chosen for these particular apparitions.

Our morning of the 18th started out with breakfast and then we immediately proceeded to the spot of the apparitions. It has been taken place at the Blue Cross at the base of Apparition Hill for some time now. The Blue Cross is where Our Lady once appeared to one of the visionaries in the early years and a cross was put up to mark the spot.

Rain was forecasted for that day and the thought was that the apparition was going to take place inside Mirjana's pansion. The weather miraculously cleared up for us this day and other days when rain was certain. Rain was not a factor despite it being forecasted for the majority of our trip. Thank you Lord!

The group got to the Blue Cross around 9am. The apparition usually takes place around 2pm. We got there early because an influx of pilgrims was expected. We were able to get an incredibly close vantage point to Mirjana. Our little group started a Rosary after an Italian group finished praying theirs in Italian. Just a short time later a small band came along and played some songs before the scheduled official Rosaries were to begin. At this point, to me, this experience became otherworldly. The recitation of the Rosary by all of us pilgrims, as the crowd began to fill in as expected, was amazing. The band also played like a Charismatic version of Kumbaya and Immaculate Mary and another song I didn't recognize in Croatian, Italian and English in between the Mysteries. The atmosphere was electric. We recited about 4 Rosaries by the time some cheers broke out in the distance as Mirjana began making her way towards the apparition spot. This was about 1:30pm or so.

Some of our group and myself were just behind the Blue Cross and the statue of Our Lady, which is there as well. We were up and to the left if you are facing the front of the cross. Film crews were set up right in front of us on both sides of the cross. Cimela was set up there as well with her video equipment.

We finally see Mirjana emerge through the crowd with Sean Bloomfield guiding her by hand. The area around the Blue Cross has some stone pews, which were occupied by special guests of Mirjana I assume. There were many priests in this roped off area as well, including Father Crotty.

The first thing I was given to "feel" and "sense" prior to Mirjana's arrival were the strong presence of the Holy Angels. I could "see" them encircling the base of Apparition Hill as though they were checking out the area. The Angels were huge with long flowing robes. I "felt" their presence many times before in the past but they seemed larger than usual this day.

Mirjana greeted all the priests before she knelt down on the rocky floor right in front of the Cross. She then joined in the recitation of the Rosary. Sean knelt right next to her on her left side. Many people were recording these very anxious and exciting moments with their cell phones including myself. Several minutes passed and Mirjana began to rock back and forth almost shivering it seemed like, which I was told was unusual. As I had my phone lifted up recording at this point, I was trying to be in the moment, meaning keeping myself in prayer. Then all of sudden, the actual feeling of being lifted off the ground hit me. It was as though I was beginning to float. I had to look down to honestly see if I was. I was not. This caught me off guard. It was a couple of minutes after that, that Our Lady appeared to Mirjana. Her back and forth and jittery motion gave way to a gasp and a look to the sky with an enormous smile on her face. I could see that she was conversing with Our Lady. I then began to "hear" the conversation but I couldn't understand the language. It seemed as though I wasn't supposed to "hear" what was being said because I had the "understanding" that it wasn't for me. It was somewhat muffled as well. I then turned my focus on Mirjana. If I wasn't supposed to "listen" in, then I wanted to see if I was able to "feel" what she was feeling. This may have been the first time perhaps, that this "Empathic Gift" from the Holy Spirit, was used in this way. I don't remember if I purposefully ever tried to "feel" a certain person's emotions on cue. Whatever the case, the Spirit of the Lord allowed me to "feel" Mirjana at that moment.

I "felt" her joy, but not at her level because again, the apparition was not meant for me per se. I did "feel" her pain at a high level though right before Our Lady left. When this hurt came to me, it was just moments before Mirjana visibly changed in her demeanor as the apparition ended. I "knew" the apparition was about to end because of what I "felt". These feelings didn't linger because like for most people there, this incredible experience was mesmerizing to all present. We all saw how drained Mirjana looked at this point as she almost collapsed. Some of the group commented later on how they felt sympathy for her. To see the whole apparition first hand and to see what she goes through, and what she's' gone through over the last 37 years, one can't help but have sympathy for her. She's a very special soul.

Our Lady's message was then dictated to Miki and to another woman as well. The message was then roughly translated and given to the crowd in Croatian, English and then Italian. The final and proper translation was released just hours later. The message given was:

"Dear children,

My earthly life was simple. I loved and I rejoiced in small things. I loved life – the gift from God – even though pain and sufferings pierced my heart.

My children, I had the strength of faith and boundless trust in God's love. All those who have the strength of faith are stronger. Faith makes you live according to what is good and then the light of God's love always comes at the desired moment. That is the strength, which sustains in pain and suffering.

My children, pray for the strength of faith, trust in the Heavenly Father, and do not be afraid. Know that not a single creature who belongs to God will be lost but will live forever. Every pain has its end and then life in freedom begins there where all of my children come – where everything is returned.

My children, your battle is difficult. It will be even more difficult, but you follow my example. Pray for the strength of faith; trust in the love of the Heavenly Father.

I am with you. I am manifesting myself to you. I am encouraging you. With immeasurable motherly love I am caressing your souls. Thank you."

What a beautiful message from the Queen of Peace.

This pilgrimage definitely made a tremendous impact on me. The call from Our Lady for me was to go deeper into prayer, to meditate deeper during the Holy Rosary and to continue to pray for souls, in particular healing. The group also played a big part in the incredible spiritual journey I was on in Medjugorje. Each one of us were called by Our Lady individually to come here, but we were called to experience this beautiful pilgrimage together.

Queen of Peace, pray for us!

Chapter 13: Dark Night Of The Soul

The "Dark Night Of The Soul", was a book written by one the great Saints of the Catholic Church, St John of the Cross.

St John was a Spanish Catholic mystic who lived in the 16th Century. He was the religious companion of another great Spanish mystic St Teresa of Avila. Both St John and St Teresa are Doctors of the Church.

A Doctor of the Church is a Saint in whom the Catholic Church has declared their writings to have contributed greatly to the theology and doctrines of the Catholic Church.

There are only 35 Doctors of the Church as of the beginning of 2018.

A very good description of what the "Dark Night of the Soul" is comes from a friend of mine named Desiree. The following are her words.

"To be in a dark night does not mean to be in a night of pain or suffering. What Saint John means when he describes this "dark night" is that one must be fully detached from worldly things, and be in a total state of uncertainty. This "dark night" compels us to walk by faith ALONE. Nothing else, just our faith. This can be frightening because in this "dark night" it may appear that God is silent and away from us. That is not the case.

When one is within this "dark night", God is putting to test their faith. He wants to see if we still trust Him even in times of total darkness.

You should be praying now more than ever. The "dark night" NEEDS those fervent prayers. Saint John tells us to view such a journey with God, like that of a mother and her child. At first, it may seem that God is always with us. This would be the mother nurturing her baby, but as the baby begins to grow, it's time for the mother to place the baby down and have it learn to walk on its own.

God wants us to walk to Him by our own faith, our own works. He cannot always baby us. We must grow in spirit and this is when we feel that God is most silent."

My journey has had its share of the "dark night".

The first instance took place in the first few months of my journey back in 2006.

I remember being at work when this abandonment "feeling" came upon me. It felt like I was left alone by the Lord. It was as though He withdrew the constant presence I had of Him up to that point. I was scared. I thought I had done something wrong to have His presence taken away from me. There was an empty "feeling" within my soul. The only knowledge I had of this "feeling" was what I had read in St Faustina's Diary. She had gone 6 months in this same state and was close to death because of it. A priest finally recognized what the Lord was allowing her to go through. He recognized that this "dark night" of hers was in preparation for her mission. The Mission of spreading the message and devotion of Divine Mercy.

I believe the Lord allowed this "dark night" of mine to commence for my own mission. It was all spiritual favors up that moment. My "babying" ended at that moment.

Many moments like this occur when the Lord has something more for me to do, "missions" as I use to call them. For instance like the "clusters" of deaths I "receive" that I wrote about in the first book. The multiple impending deaths that I "receive" at a single moment. The "dark night" prepares me to be able to discern and pray and to get through the "clusters".

At times of spiritual progression, the "dark night" will begin as well. After these extended periods, I "receive" an understanding of this progression. It's nothing of my doing though; it's all the Holy Spirit. This is not to say than I'm holy or anything like that; it's just my surrendering to God to allow Him to work through me. I surrender everything to His Holy will.

I know the periods I've gone through were difficult. St Faustina's 6 months, to me is remarkable but St Teresa of Calcutta's 50 years without feeling the Lord is mind-blowing.

In her letters that were made public after her passing, she writes about the "darkness". Many theologians have said that her case is the longest "dark night of the soul" they have ever encountered. To accomplish all that she did, and to help as many people as she did in this "dark" state is truly incredible. St Teresa of Calcutta, pray for us!

I truly recommend St John's book on this matter. "The Dark Night Of The Soul" should be required reading for everyone who is serious about their faith and spiritual growth. St Teresa of Avila's books should be essential to every Catholic as well. "Interior Castles" and "The Way to Perfection" are on top of the list.

I believe many Catholics are unaware how the Lord works in us in this "dark night". We are "trained" from very early on that the spiritual life is all sunshine and rainbow feelings. It isn't until we truly get serious about our faith that this "new life" comes about. We must truly surrender to God's will and allow the Holy Spirit to mold us as a master sculptor molds clay into a masterpiece.

"The endurance of darkness is the preparation for great light."-St John of the Cross

Chapter 14: Dream Visions

The form of visions that I am given that are the least common, is what I call "Dream Visions".

These "dream visions" are visions that occur in the moments between being awake and of falling asleep. It appears as though I'm still awake but the visions are in a dream state. It's almost like being in a lucid dream but what's being "shown" to me is something that will come to pass. I'm able to see all of my surrounding in this state and see all the details of this vision with great recall.

These visions have marked some significant moments in my family's life. In a way, I lived through these moments twice, once in these visions and once in real life.

The first of these visions, occurred after lunch on a Thursday in 2006. As I've written before, we work in the mornings and then again in the late afternoons and into the evening in our family business of carpet cleaning and janitorial services. I usually take a nap after lunch before we have to start up again in the late afternoons. I usually take a nap on my recliner that I have in my bedroom. In the state of falling asleep during the first occurrence, I see a member of the prayer group I attended at the time. This member, a young man in his 20's or early 30's, had a wife and some young children. In this vision, we are in our prayer group meeting on our typical Thursday night, and he is seated to the right of me. He turns to me and his eyes are of greenish color, like he had an evil spirit within him. His demeanor matched the evil presence that began to fill my senses like it typically does when I'm given to "feel" evilness around. He starts walking towards me as fear has enveloped my whole body at this point. I suddenly snap out of this state with the same sensations of the "dream visions". The fear and the "feeling" of evilness felt all too real.

That night at the prayer group, the young man and his wife are there and they are seated to the right of me like in the vision. I immediately remember the whole vision as I see him sit down in his chair. There were a lot of people there that night, and typically new members such as myself at the time and this couple, usually don't have a regular place to sit and so for us to be seated like we were that night like the vision, was eerily strange to me right away. When we got to the deeper part of prayer during our meeting, this young man turned to me like the vision; the same look he gave me in the vision came to pass. My heart was racing at that point because I fully expected him to start walking towards me. I "felt" the same evilness lurking about but the young man didn't approach me. After the prayer meeting, one of my sisters, "received" during that time that this young man was in desperate need of prayers. My sister wanted to go pray for him but didn't because she felt it wasn't proper for her to do so. She rarely if ever did that, and so that's why she didn't. I believe what I "received" in the "dream vision" was the Lord showing me that this young man was in need of more personal deeper prayer. I was too focused on what had occurred to recognize that at the time. It was only after my sister recounted what she had "received" that I understood that.

This occurrence was very early on in my journey and I was still incredibly overwhelmed with everything that I was "receiving" at the time. It's only by the Holy Spirit that have I grown since then. I still pray for this young man and his wife to this day 12 years later. I found out later after they had moved away not long after that night, that he and his wife had separated.

Another one of these visions occurred in the middle of 2008. It was the same as the first one but this time it was a little different. The lucid part of these visions, when I'm able to control and observe began with this particular vision.

Like the first instance in 2006, I was in the same in-between state when this vision occurred.

In an instant, I was at the entrance of my hometown chapel of Our Lady of Lourdes. I'm aware that I'm not in my bedroom anymore and I begin to look around my surroundings trying to figure out how I got there. I look down and I see I'm carrying a baby carrier in my right hand. I then see one of my sisters standing next to me as I'm hold this baby. Someone else is standing to my right but I didn't look at them as something else got my attention. I notice a priest at the front of the Church at the altar just waiting. I couldn't tell who he was as we were at the rear of the Church. As I'm examining the altar from where I'm standing, I was snapped back into reality and I was back in my bedroom bewildered to what just occurred. It was very surreal to say the least.

I immediately wrote down what I had just "received" as

I use to do back in those days. I contemplated on the vision for some time and then I moved on and left it to God's will for whatever reason I was "shown" this event.

A few months later, my first great-nephew Dominic was going to be baptized in the Church. My oldest niece Tia, his mom, chose my sister Maria and I to be his Godparents.

We took the required Baptism class shortly before the Sacrament took place on a Saturday morning.

The whole family showed up on this late Summer morning for Dominic's Baptism. I was excited, as this was the first time I was chosen to be someone's Godparent. My spiritual journey being still somewhat new at that point, made this great day even more exciting for me.

Leading up to this day, I kind of expected to "receive" something supernatural at the Baptism because I was "receiving" so much at that point that I figured that the Lord was going to allow that. Perhaps even "seeing" the Holy Spirit descending down on Dominic like when the Holy Spirit descended on Our Lord at His Baptism.

As some of my family began to enter the Chapel, my niece and her husband arrived at the Church. Dom as we call him, was only 6 months old at the time. My sister and I went to go greet my niece and help her with Dom as they got out of the car right in front of the Chapel. I believe my niece's mom, my ex-sister in law, had the baby carrier with Dom in it. I take the carrier from her to help her as it looked like she was struggling with it. We then enter the Church and at that moment, the "dream vision" I "received" months earlier became reality. I looked down and saw the baby in the carrier in my right hand and my sister Maria next to me exactly like vision. I was taken aback at that moment. I looked up towards the altar and I see our priest at the time waiting for us. Everything came to pass exactly. I was very conscious of this as we all walked to the front for the beginning of the Sacrament.

I don't why I received this specific event in my family's life. Was it to show me that this particular "gift" was and still is present within me? Whatever reason, I'm thankful for it. Perhaps someday the Lord will reveal to me the reason. The supernatural that I was expecting beforehand did occur though but not as I expected.

Within a year another "dream vision" took place and came to pass. This time it was at the birth of one my nieces.

Same drill as before, the dream/awake state, the contemplation and then leaving it to God.

To be honest, I was really curious at this point because of the question of whose birth was I being "shown".

The difference with this "dream vision" and the others, was the length of the vision. This vision was so brief that I didn't have time to look around at my surroundings. The few things I was given to "see" were a hospital room and me standing at the foot of the bed with 2 people and both side of me. I also saw a woman in the bed but her identity I couldn't make out because by that time the vision had ended. It seemed to have lasted only a few seconds.

The "dream vision" came to pass with the birth of my niece Mary Grace. The vision came to my mind the moment I walked into the crowded room and stood at the foot of the bed. I saw the 2 people and both sides of me and the woman in the bed, which ended up being one of my sister in-laws. I made this revelation to my sister who was standing next me at that moment. She said to jump and down to change the vision from taken place exactly in real life. I laughed and I jokingly jumped up and down a few times. Once again I was taken aback by this event coming to pass.

Again, why was I shown this? I leave it God. He will answer me in His time.

The other "dream visions", which I wrote about in the previous chapter of "Healing", was also another significant event in my life.

The most profound of these visions came in late 2016, in which of this writing has not come to pass. The vision was so clear, that I was able to wake up and go back into it a couple of times. I was able to fall back into this dream/awake state on cue. I was able to very clearly see every little detail of my surroundings including all the people involved.

This vision began similar to the one of my niece being born. The setting was a hospital room. The room was lit by the sun shining through the window that was to the right of the hospital bed. I see a close friend of mine in the bed and she had just given birth. She was still sweaty from the delivery and her hair was a mess and she looked tired but happy. She was holding the newborn baby. My thinking was at that moment that it was a little girl. I see my family on both sides of the bed. I see my dad and my mom and my brothers and sisters there. The strange thing was that my friend's family wasn't in the room. I quickly as I'm going in and out of this vision, start looking for myself. At first I believed this whole vision was playing out like I was watching a movie because my perspective was of me watching this from a position away from everyone. I then realized that I was there in real time just observing this scene. At that point, I snapped back to the present with a "what did I just see?!" reaction.

This vision was bothering me for many months afterwards. I finally went to my priest Father Balaji in the Summer of 2017 to get some spiritual direction on it.

Father Balaji said to me that this vision could have different meanings. One meaning he said, was that my family and myself being there, meant that my friend that was the focus of the vision would need our support in the future. Another meaning he said was that perhaps my friend was possibly going to stray from her spiritual path that she was on and get pregnant. In any case he said, my friend needed my support and guidance, as she was a new in the Faith.

I truly believe that this is a future event that involves my family. A birth to be exact. "Who's birth?" is still my question after almost 2 years. Perhaps my friend is just representing someone else in the vision. That's happened many times before in prophetic dreams I have "received" from the Lord. I leave it to the Lord and

His Divine Providence. I struggle at times overanalyzing visions, I know I need to work on that. I pray that the Lord corrects me on this fault.

There is a quote from a movie about Saint Padre Pio that I love, in it he says, "God has a notebook and every once in a while He lets me look at it". I feel that these "dream visions" are just like that, He lets me look into His grand notebook from time to time. It's an incredible grace that He has granted me.

Chapter 15: Our Lady

Since my Medjugorje pilgrimage, my prayer life has intensified. The refocus on the Rosary in particular has been what's stood out to me. In the beginning of my journey with Our Lady, I would meditate very deeply on the Mysteries while praying the most Holy Rosary. After many years of daily Rosaries, the meditation part began to wane. There were days were the meditation was strong but the focus was definitely not what it was. The renewal of the love of the Rosary has been re-ignited in my soul. I'm praying all 20 Mysteries most days now since my trip.

The interior locutions I "receive" from Our Lady have become a regular occurrence again and not sporadic like it had been. I took those early days of the locutions for granted. I know now what an incredible grace I have been given by Our Lady.

I had a dream in the early years of the locutions where Our Lord gave me to "know" that I was one of the people who were given the grace to "see" and "hear" Our Lady.

In this particular dream, I'm in an open field at night and I'm running towards a heavily wooded area. Everything was illuminated by a huge "Super Moon". I stop running as I notice several others running towards the wooded area as well. Two other people stop with me and one of them, a young woman, asks the other, who's also a woman, a question. "Why is everyone running towards the trees?". The other woman then said to her, "these are the only people in the world who can "see" and "hear" the Virgin Mary". With that, we all start running towards "Mary". I woke up with an incredible peace in my heart. This confirmed to me all that I had been given by Our Lady, the visions, the locutions and the messages. I did some research after this dream and found out that the Moon, is a symbol of Our Lady. The Sun, is Jesus and the light from Him illuminates the Moon, Mary. That why the "Super Moon" in the dream, because she was calling us and we were running towards her.

A few days later, I read an article on a Catholic online site about a young African girl who says that she receives visions and locutions from Our Lady. The young woman says that there are some people who just "hear" Our Lady and others who both "see" and "hear" Our Lady. "Wow!", I immediately thought. This confirmed my dream. I have been truly blessed with this incredible and rare gift of "seeing" and "hearing" the Mother of God!

The article also stated that thousands gathered every month to witness this young woman "receiving" apparitions of Our Lady.

This reminded me of the prophecy I wrote about in my first book about the Blessed Mother. The prophecy about Our Lady "coming" to my hometown of Mineral Wells, Texas, where people would be coming from all over for Her. The curious and believers all will come to my hometown seeking Her like in Lourdes, Fatima and Medjugorje.

In February of 2018, Our Prayer Garden and Grotto at Our Lourdes Catholic Church was officially dedicated by our Bishop of the Diocese of Ft Worth, Texas, Michael Olson. This beautiful prayer garden has a small Grotto with a flowing fountain. A statue of Our Lady is prominently place here. The garden also has The Stations of The Cross and a beautiful Crucifix within the grounds. Engraved bricks pave some of walking areas of the garden as well. My family has a few bricks there including one honoring the memory of my brother Juan.

The dedication was set up to coincide with the feast day of Our Lady of Lourdes. After a beautiful Mass, the Bishop and Father Balaji and about 4 or 5 more priests from the area and the whole church processed with candles to the Prayer Garden. The huge statue of Our Lady was carried in the procession to the Garden. This incredible sight was exactly like the profound vision I had in 2015. Like the vision, the entire procession filled the streets adjacent to the Church. The candles and the statue were exactly the same as the vision. My heart was bursting with joy seeing how this entire scene was coming to pass like I was "shown" a few years earlier. This was further confirmation on this prophecy that I had long been given. It was continuing to unfold on this beautiful night.

The dedication was held on a Friday night and 2 days later on a Sunday afternoon, I went to the Prayer Garden again to pray my Rosary and to give thanks and to meditate on what had occurred just 2 days earlier.

Some miraculous Lourdes water was poured into the flowing water fountain of the Grotto during the dedication and so I blessed myself with it as I prayed.

In contemplating the vision and what occurred just a couple of days earlier, the "inspiration" to have weekly Rosaries at the Garden came to me. I immediately texted Father Balaji and asked if this was something we could do. He quickly responded and said that it was a very good idea and he gave his approval. I was excited! Thank you Holy Virgin!

I posted the announcement of the first Rosary on the Church's social media page for the following Sunday evening at 6:30pm.

As that Sunday approached, I kept reflecting on the prophecy. I believe that this new Prayer Garden is what Our Lady wanted as well. I was only "shown" pieces of this prophecy throughout the 10 years that I was first given to "know" what was coming. A major part of what I was "given", was that of Our Lady asking for a true devotion to the Holy Rosary from us. This message is nothing new but she was asking this specifically from us, the parishioners of Our Lady of Lourdes. Having weekly Rosaries in the Garden was a great way to begin that devotion. She also asked a long time ago for written prayer petitions. She said she would intercede for us for whatever we had written down and prayed for during these Rosaries. With that in mind, I made a petition box and placed it in front of the statue of Our Lady. I had small pieces of paper and pens ready for anyone that wanted to place a petition in front of her.

We started the first Rosary around 6:30pm. There were about 12 of us there including Father Balaji and Father James, one of our new associate priests. I gave an introduction before the actual Rosary began. We had brought some more miraculous Lourdes water to be poured into the fountain. The Rosary went well on this cold February night. The in-ground lights that illuminated the Garden, made the atmosphere even more prayerful. I "felt" Our Lady's presence very strongly there. I "saw" her with her arms outstretched towards us. My mother also "felt" Our Lady and also "saw" her for a short moment. That was my confirmation on what I "saw". It was a very beautiful night. We were truly blessed by the Mother of God!

I wasn't sure if the people there were open to coming every week and so after Father B blessed the intentions, I said that I hoped we could continue praying as we did this night every Sunday after this. Everyone there agreed that we should. That made me ecstatic in knowing that this new but prophesied journey was truly beginning.

On the subsequent Sunday we had some more people come as it was announced after both the English and Spanish Mass. We topped out around 30 people in the first couple of months despite numerous announcements. The average attendance was around 20 people per Sunday. It became disappointing not having more people participate as the weeks rolled on. I felt this building pressure within me in not revealing to the faithful who were there, what I had and still was "receiving" from Our Lady.

I know in one of the earlier Rosaries that we had, I "heard" Our Lady say that her heart was full. I could "feel" her presence and her love as she spoke these words. At the time, I was reading Mirjana's, the visionary from Medjugorje, book. That night after the Rosary I came upon a message in the book from Our

Lady that was given some time ago and it was exactly what I "heard" this night, "my heart is full". I was so happy knowing that once again I was given confirmation on what I "received".

I spoke to the Rosary group about my pilgrimage to Medjugorje the first Sunday I returned home. I wanted what I "experienced" there, to begin in my hometown. I started playing music before and after the Rosaries before I left, but what I wanted was music to played live like they did in Medjugorje. The Rosaries came alive when they played music in-between each Mysteries over there. I envisioned that here. Having such a little turnout as we had, it wasn't something that was available to us aside from learning to play instruments ourselves. I didn't want to ask any parishioners who did play instruments, who weren't attending these Rosaries because I didn't want them to feel forced or obligated to be there. If they want to play for Our Lady, it must come from their heart to do so.

Finally after much prayer and "receiving" multiple locutions from Our Lady, I "knew" I had to tell our faithful group what I had been "receiving".

I had "received" from Our Lady a message in the middle of April for someone who was on the pilgrimage to Medjugorje with me. Along with that as well, I "received" confirmation that Our Lady wanted the Rosaries to be like it had been in those early years of these locutions. That involved invoking her presence while praying the Rosary and letting the people know that she was there and "speaking" to me. I was a little hesitant but this interior pressure was getting too much for me to handle. I had to tell the faithful. The only question was how to do it.

On the last Sunday of April, Our Lady during the Rosary instructed me to tell the faithful. I hinted about it before the Rosary began but I failed to tell them. It wasn't until Our Lady "appeared" to me and instructed me, that the fear to tell them left me. As the final song of "Ave Maria" ended marking the end of the Rosary, I began to tell them a shortened version of the prophecy of 2008. I told them that Our Lady had "appeared" to me this night and wanted them to know that she was there among us. I told them that she had appeared as Our Lady of Fatima this night and that she took in all our petitions. It appeared to me that our Guardian Angels took the petitions and handed them to her. The Angels appeared as small children. They seemed to be around 6 or 7 years old. Her presence was as strong as I've ever felt it during these 2 months of holding these weekly Rosaries. I started breaking down a bit recounting all that had occurred. I've told the prophecy that I wrote about in great detail in my first book multiple times, but this account was different. I guess it was because I had just gone through this incredible "experience" and then immediately telling the faithful about it for the first time. They all took it in with great faith. Several of them had tears rolling down their cheeks as I told them about the great blessings we had received. "Our Lady blessed us all", I said to them. They all came up to me individually right before they left thanking me for my testimony.

I was so relieved that I was given the grace to recount the "experience" that night. I pray that Our Lady will continue to bless us with her apparitions here. I believe the people will come and will be converted and be blessed as the prophecy goes. She will in turn lead us to Her Son Our Lord Jesus Christ. Thank you Queen of Peace!

Chapter 16: Prayer

St Padre Pio once said, "prayer is oxygen for the soul", and after 12 years on this journey, that quote is very accurate.

The extent of my prayer life in my prior life consisted of a quick Sign of the Cross before bed. I would occasionally pray a little more if I needed something. The desire to pray more came when my conversion first began in 2006. I built up my prayer life fairly quick from that point. The supernatural that came at the inception of my conversion was the reason I was given the grace to pray as I did.

In reading about the lives of the Saints, I was fascinated with their prayer life. I thought, "what separates the way they pray and the way others pray, and the way I pray?". I wanted to pray as they did, not because of pride but because I wanted to love God as much as they did. This burning desire to pray for souls has always been strong since the beginning. When I knew that my prayers were helping in the salvation of souls, especially for the dying, this desire burned even greater in my soul. It's a fire that's never flickered. Praise be to God for that!

My fascination with the way that people around me whom I knew prayed piqued my interest as well.

I was exposed to the many ways that people prayed by my experiences in the prayer group. It seemed like only the older Hispanic women who didn't work were the ones who prayed a little more than the people who worked full time. The older Hispanic woman have always been very prayerful, I know that by seeing my paternal grandmother praying the Rosary constantly.

During a youth conference workshop for adults, I learned how my prayer life was compared to my peers.

In this workshop that was held by a priest who later became bishop, asked this packed room of about 75 other youth ministers about our prayer life. He asked, "How many of you pray at least 30 minutes a day?" and about 90-95% of the people there raised their hands including myself. He then asked "1 hour of prayer a day?"; about 10-15% of the hands went up including mine. Then when he asked an hour and a half and then 2 hours a day, my hand was the only one up in this large hotel meeting room. I had my hand up a little sheepishly because I was surprised that my hand was the only one up. The priest looked around to see whose hands were still up at the point. He didn't see mine though but the people around me did. I got some surprised looks from them.

The reason I was able to pray for such a long time was because I was able to pray while I worked. Being in the family business of carpet cleaning and janitorial service allowed me the freedom to pray while working. I've prayed a ton of Rosaries over the years while vacuuming the various local businesses we've cleaned on a daily basis.

My prayers just grew as well as I kept remembering people to pray for. It wasn't enough to pray for a person once; I felt that I had to pray them everyday. I made a prayer list of the names of all the people that I could remember. I wrote down old classmates, people from the janitorial work that we did and anyone else who I had ever had contact with. I still pray for that list daily. Then there came another group of people I began to list daily. These were people whom I've met since the beginning of my conversion. This list is not written down, it's by memory. These are people in whom I've had a "connection" with whether they realized or not.

It got so exhausting praying daily for so many people by name, that I tried to get a priestly dispensation from it. I told a priest about my dilemma and he just said that it was good that I prayed for them by name. When I read that someone once asked Padre Pio why he prayed for so many people by name and not just a general prayer for them as a group, he responded that each person needed to be presented to God individually. That gave me a renewed fervor in praying for people by their individual name. I needed to present them to God one by one. I truly believe that wants He wants me to do. It's only by His grace that I can. I truly believe that He also allows me to truly "connect" spiritually with everyone I pray for. In my experience, people take comfort when they know that someone outside of their families is praying for them. I believe in many cases, I'm the only one praying for them at all. I feel a great responsibility in praying for people. I know that's one of the things I'm called to do in this life of mine.

A promise that I make to all my Confirmation classes is that I will pray for them for the rest of my days and once a week now, I do so. I've had 9 classes as of 2018 and I remember every student and pray for them by name. That's probably around 250 souls as of this book. I do get tired on occasion praying for each precious soul by name but apart from God's grace, the desire to save souls drives me to do this daily.

My overall prayers are structured, meaning each day I pray in a certain order. I begin my day with prayer. The very first thing I do when I get up is pray. I start with thanking God for a new day and then I ask the Blessed Mother for her prayers and then St Joseph's. I then pray to the Holy Arch-Angels for their protection and then the Angel's and then my Guardian Angel's. I end with my prayers to the Holy Saints and Blessed Souls in Heaven for their intercessions.

I then make and offering to The Holy Trinity in thanksgiving which consists of multiple Our Fathers and the Apostles Creed. I then invoke the Holy Spirit to guide me and to grant me the necessary "gifts" needed to help pray for souls. I continue with praying for some personal intentions of my own and then the long list of intercessions begins. In the same order as before but in a more detailed aspect. I pray to Our Lord as I begin with my family and to those who are in need of prayer. It's prayers for the Church, for our leaders and for all those who are most abandoned. I pray for the addicted, the imprisoned, the lost, the unborn, the suffering and for many more. They are all prayed for everyday. Then the individual and different intentions continue on down to the Holy Virgin, St Joseph and so forth in more detail.

The afternoon usually begins with multiple Rosaries for various intentions and then I pray the Chaplet of Divine

Mercy. I sometimes add a second Chaplet if there's a "special" need for it. I also try to visit the Chapel as much as I can during the week and pray for some intentions there as well.

Daily Mass is also a part of my weekly schedule. That's very important in sustaining my prayer life. Receiving the Holy Eucharist daily is essential to my spiritual life. Everything I do stems from receiving the Body and Blood of Our Lord Jesus. Without that, I'm lost.

I finish my day with a quick rundown of the Heavenly Court's intercessions again but with prayers of thanksgiving added once more. I pray for the Holy Souls in Purgatory and I pray for the dying as well,

I will do some prayers emphasizing some intentions before bed most of time as well. I then do an examination of conscience and I pray for forgiveness and then my day ends.

I've added fasting and daily Scripture reading since I've come back from my pilgrimage to Medjugorje. These new elements have been very beneficial to my spiritual life as well.

When I pray with a group of people now, usually before a Confirmation class begins and ends and the same with the Youth Group meetings, I pray vocally but with limited "depth". I know if I do pray with fervor on these occasions, this incredible supernatural element would open up and so I limit my prayers. These are not occasions that call for this type of prayer. Also, it would be too much for me to take in if I did that on every prayer occasion. The same goes for Mass, I limit the "depth" that I go into because of the same reason. I do not want to open myself up to whatever would come from a large gathering of people.

When I had less control over these things, too much "stuff" would come in and I would be a mess. Perhaps I lose some graces during Mass by closing myself off like this but only God knows such things.

St Paul says we should pray without ceasing and I hope I'm getting close to doing that. I believe the Lord has led me to this prayer life of mine. It's nothing of my doing. I never liked the term "Prayer Warrior". Prayer Warrior seems to suggest that a person is praying far and beyond what everyone else is doing. We are all called to pray with great fervor and devotion. These "warriors" are doing just that. We are all the same. We all have the power of prayer.

I hope in writing about my prayer life, someone will be inspired to pray more than they are now. I hope they will discover the great joy that comes from prayer but most importantly, I hope their relationship with Our Lord and the Heavenly court blossoms because of it.

Chapter 17: The Dark Side

Since my last writing, the type of evilness that I have "experienced" as I wrote about in the first book has actually decreased but it still rears its ugly head from time to time. The first 10 years were extraordinary. I'm not sure why the decrease of that type of activity but that's definitely ok with me.

I still get the occasional evil presence that invades my dreams to the point where I have to get up and bless my bedroom and the house. My dream state is my most vulnerable state and so I figure that's why I get attacked there. The feelings I get during the moments haven't changed. The cold, shivering, fearful, and chills throughout my body are still there. My mind and spirit fight what my body is feeling and I'm able by God's grace to fight through it fairly quick.

Perhaps one of the reasons the demonic activity has decreased is my lack of focus on it. The times when I do focus on it is when someone speaks to me or to someone close to me in an ill way, and it's out of character for them. I then can "sense" an evil influence within them or around them. I can't tell the person what I'm "sensing" with them at that moment because that would just upset them more. I just politely nod my head or I just try to diffuse the situation by deflecting the conversation on whatever they're speaking wrongly about. If they only knew what I was given to "see" and "feel" within them in those moments, they would shake with fear and apologize profusely. I just pray for them during these moments. It does upset me but I understand. We allow this evil influence in by letting our guard down. The evil one is very sharp in terms of finding our weaknesses and prodding us until we give him room to enter. I learned this from one of St. Teresa of Avila's books. She tells us to always be on alert for the Evil One and his minions as they try to pervade us constantly. As I've written before, we allow this evil to enter via our senses. I've told my Confirmation classes and many others, on what is appropriate to watch in terms of movies and TV shows. I tell them, "Imagine that Jesus Himself is physically sitting right next to you watching this particular show or movie, would you still watch it?". A lot of times the youths I tell this to take a long pause in answering because they don't see these situations in these terms. I tell that Jesus is next to them in these instances even though they can't see Him.

I prayed a Rosary with some youths from our parish in the middle of 2018, which I hadn't done in awhile, and could "see" the evilness that was scurrying about amongst them. These youths had allowed this darkness to enter their lives but they were oblivious to it. I use to "see" this many times with many adults during my years in the prayer group. I think cell phones and social media have made this evil influence an epidemic upon our world.

One of things that a priest said during his talk while I was in Medjugorje was that when he was 16 years old and had gone to Confession that the priest read his soul and told him his sins. He said that the sins that this priest was calling off to him, weren't sins to his 16 year old self. He didn't see that the bad things he was doing was wrong. I believe that's another big issue within our world. Many people do not think what they're doing is wrong. That's why the line to Communion is long and the line to Confession is very, very short.

A young woman from one my early Confirmation classes once asked me, "What if I don't feel sorry for what I'm doing?" I told her that there was something wrong with that if we didn't realize or care that we were offending God by those sins. It all stems from parenting. I read a comment from a priest who said that we could have the best priests, the best homilies, the best catechesis and the best teachers, and it wouldn't do much good if these youths didn't have the spiritual support and foundation from their parents. We can only do so much.

A speaker at a middle school rally held at a Catholic High School in early 2017 said to the youths, "Look at your top 3 friends, are they getting you closer to Christ or pulling you away from Christ? If they are pulling you away from Christ, get new friends. Pray for them, but get new friends. If they are doing bad things, chances are great that you will be doing bad things as well." He is right and unfortunately good kids get caught up with those doing bad things. Peer pressure is at an all-time high. One just had to see the nightly news to see this being true.

The solution is prayer, the Sacraments and Mass. We must be fortified by the Sacraments to protect ourselves from the demonic. The Rosary is a powerful weapon as well.

The reason the evil spirits are scurrying about during prayer is similar to what happens in Medjugorje quite frequently, the presence of Our Lord and Our Lady. I've heard the same awful cries during Adoration during my time in the Charismatic Renewal. Evilness can't stand the presence of something holy.

As I wrote about earlier in the chapter on Medjugorje, the demonic fear Our Lady. That's why one hears the demonic cries from some of the people there when Our Lady appears to the visionaries during a public apparition. The Rosary with some of the youths that we had made the evil spirits scramble with fear because of Our Lady. These youths weren't possessed by any means but they did have a strong influence of evil spirits around them. I know the Rosary has some benefits for them that night, I just hope they continue praying on their own. Perhaps we need to start praying the Rosary with them more frequently in order to get them accustomed to Our Lady and her graces from Above.

Again, the more usual type of evilness and darkness, which I'm given to "feel" now, is that which I have just described, the demonic influence.

The Texas school shooting, the Las Vegas massacre, the suicide bombers, the suicide downed planes, all have the same demonic influences. That's what I'm given to "feel" the most in terms of the darkness. I pray that we all turn to God and His Mercy. If not, the demonic activity will increase and these tragedies will continue but at an increased rate. God have mercy on us!

Chapter 18: Final Thoughts

In writing these 2 books about my long journey in the Supernatural, it feels as though I'm writing about some mythological figure. I can understand how it would be hard for a non-believer to fathom everything I've written about. I'm sure some believers also have some difficulties believing these testimonies as well.

I believe it's because a lot of people think that miracles and these supernatural events were limited to the time that Christ walked the Earth. Some people who have knowledge of the Saints perhaps think that these occurrences only happened with them as well. I know I didn't have any knowledge of it aside from the Biblical stories I grew up with. Whatever the case, the Lord working through His people is still very prevalent today.

I believe as Dr Macnutt does as he wrote in his book about healing, he said that the Church needs to go back to the time when the Church grew exponentially. That was the time when miracles and the supernatural were rampant among the early Church. Those miracles are still happening today! The Church has gone away from that in terms of miraculous healings, supernatural events and otherworldly phenomenon from Above. Dr Macnutt wrote that we Catholics are hungry for the supernatural. That's the reason that millions of people flock to Lourdes, Fatima and Medjugorje year in and year out. For whatever reasons the Church, outside of these holy places, have distanced itself from the supernatural. I don't know if the average Catholic truly understands that a miracle takes place at every Mass, the changing of bread and wine to the actual Body and Blood of Our Lord! I read somewhere that a non-Catholic man had said that he didn't believe that the Eucharist was really the Body and Blood of Our Lord. His reasoning was that if it was truly so, that us Catholics would constantly be prostrated and very reverent knowing that Jesus was truly present in the Tabernacle. He said from his view, we act like He's not there and so he doesn't believe. He has a good point. We don't act like we should when we enter a Catholic Church. I'm guilty of that as well from time to time. If Jesus appeared in His human form to all of us at every Mass, then we all would act accordingly as we should. Again Lourdes, Fatima, and Medjugorje are the exception in my experience. The Masses in these holy sites are very, very reverent. There's a link because of the supernatural in these places. Mineral Wells or any other parish around the World can be Lourdes, Fatima, and Medjugorje. Our Lord is present in this supernatural way in every parish not just in these places. The supernatural can happen and is happening all around us in our own Catholic Churches. My stories in these 2 books of mine are testimony to that!

We must pray for the Holy Father and all the religious around the World in particular our Bishops and priests. We must pray that the Holy Spirit will guide them in recognizing the miracles and wonders that are happening within each of our parishes. We then all will truly know that God is still working among us.

We on our part must pray and discern on what are missions are. What mission has the Lord has called you to?

I know my calling is to teach and to pray for souls and to give testimony to God's Divine Mercy.

In my years of teaching Confirmation, I've seen that the majority of the candidates, who've come through my class, have been programmed by the World to follow its calling and not the Lord's. It's safe to say that it's not just limited to the youth. I was once guilty of that as well. The World tells us that we need to be successful in its ways in order for us to be important. God is just an afterthought if even that much in the World's way of thinking. To break this way of thinking, we must pray often and "listen" to Him and be faithful in receiving the Sacraments. The Lord will speak to us and reveal our mission to us by His Spirit. We have to be open, not just our minds but our hearts as well. The Lord just asks to enter our hearts, He will do the rest after that.

St Louis de Montfort said "in order to consecrate ourselves perfectly to Our Lord, we must consecrate ourselves perfectly to Virgin Mary". The Blessed Mother is the surest way of knowing her Son perfectly. We must follow Our Lady's example in the interior life. She was the one who followed the will of Our Lord perfectly. Her words at the "Wedding at Cana", "do whatever He tells you", sums up that point. She will lead us to Him.

"Our hearts are restless, until they rest in You Lord"; this famous quote by St Augustine is still very relevant today as it was in his time. We are all searching for God, regardless of what your beliefs are. The restlessness of those who are still "blind" in the their search for Our Lord is why drug use, alcohol abuse, and sexual transgressions are at an all-time high. We seek to satisfy this restlessness with sin, which is detrimental to our souls. This false happiness is not true joy. The soul of someone in this state confuses a temporary high or temporary pleasure as happiness. Interiorly they are a mess. It's only by God's grace and the prompting of the Holy Spirit, that souls in this harmful state begin their true search for happiness, which lies in Christ alone.

This is very common in my experience. Reading the lives of some Saints with their Charism of "reading of souls" and my own experience with this Charism, solidify this point. I've been given to "feel" many souls in this harmful state despite their false facade of happiness that fool most people and many times even fooling themselves.

God is merciful. Whatever the condition of the soul, He is waiting for us with His arms outstretched ready to embrace us with His Divine Mercy. We must turn to His Mercy if we truly seek happiness.

I will end with a final story. This story was told to us while we were still in the ICU waiting room right after my brother passed away.

There was a Hispanic man who was also in grave condition in the ICU and whose family was in the large waiting room as well anxiously awaiting news on their loved one. We knew this family, as the one who relayed the following story was a lifelong friend of my brother.

By the mercy of God this Hispanic man recovered from his coma and was able to communicate with his family. He told them of a dream that he had while he was in his coma. In the dream he said, he saw another Hispanic man walking alongside of him on a beach. They approached a bridge in which the man walking with him crossed over to the other side. He said that he couldn't crossover for some reason. The other man continued on but he stayed like it wasn't his time to cross this bridge. His family told him of my brother, who was in the same ICU but that he had passed away a short time earlier.

The meaning of this "dream" is that the Lord was showing us all, that my brother crossed over to Eternity while this man was given more time on Earth. This man was given more time in this life by the Mercy of Lord. Perhaps there were things he needed to atone for. My brother's time on this Earth was up. He crossed over to Our Lord and His Divine Mercy.

I hope and pray that the testimonies in these 2 books of mine have given hope and inspiration to some people. The hope that so many are searching for. That is the hope that the Lord loves us and is truly with us and is spreading His Divine Mercy all over the world.

Jesus, I Trust In You!

Acknowledgments

I would like to give thanks once again to the Lord God for the grace of allowing me to write this second book. Without Him, it would've not been possible. I would like to thank the Blessed Mother for her constant intercession as well. Immaculate Heart of Mary, pray for us! Queen of Peace pray for us!

I would like to thank my family and friends for their love and support.

I would like to thank the "My Heart Will Triumph" group for their support and friendship.

I would like to give a special thanks to Marcos Loredo (cover model) and Armando Loredo Jr. for their help with my cover. I also would like to thank Yaretzi Ciprian for being my model for the back cover.

Thank you to Lucy Bustos for once again being my beta-reader. I really appreciated your input.

Thank you to Father Balaji and the parishioners of Our Lady of Lourdes Catholic Church in Mineral Wells, Texas.

Thank you to Juana and Desiree for your contributions as well.

Jesus, I Trust In You!